WINDOWS 98
INTERACTIVE LEARNING

Stuart Rosen

PONDVIEW
PRODUCTIONS

Published by
Pondview Productions, Inc.
7085 Shady Oak Road
Minneapolis, MN 55344

Windows 98 Interactive Learning
Published by
Pondview Productions, Inc.
7085 Shady Oak Road
Minneapolis, MN 55344

Project management: Michael Koch
Design and layout: Bookmakers

ISBN: 1-56893-920-5
Library of Congress Catalog Card Number: 98-85702
Printed in the United States of America
98 99 00   10 9 8 7 6 5 4 3 2 1

CONTENTS AT A GLANCE

CONTENTS

· ·

ACKNOWLEDGMENTS

Grateful acknowledgement is given to all who made this book possible: Amy Boxrud, who assisted in the writing; Michael Koch, project manager; Susan Glinert, who designed and typeset the book, and the team from Pondview Productions—Shel Mann, Scott Grieve, Mike McClure, Chris Smith, and John Golden.

ABOUT THE AUTHOR

Stuart Rosen has been a technical writer since 1987. The former Senior Designer/Writer at LEARN PC (later Gartner Group Learning), a leading producer of video and multi-media computer training, Stuart has created print, video, and interactive instructional materials for nearly all the major PC programs. In addition, Stuart has written HR training documentation, medical product instructions, and home improvement programs for cable television. He lives in Minneapolis, Minnesota, where he spends his free time writing and directing for the stage.

INTRODUCTION

Welcome to *Windows 98 Interactive Learning*! This book is an easy-to-use quick reference guide, designed to be a companion to the CompuWorks Interactive Learning CD-ROM. My objective is to give you clear, concise, task-oriented instructions across a broad range of Windows 98 features, plus additional reference material to help you understand Windows 98 and develop the skills to make the most of it. In short, I want you to be up and running on Windows 98 without a lot of time and trouble, getting the benefits of Windows 98 when you work, and when you play.

HOW TO USE THIS BOOK

The first part of the book takes you through the fundamentals of the Windows 98 operating system. Chapter 1 provides an overview, and addresses the different levels of Windows experience that you might have. Chapter 2 is a thorough exploration of the Windows 98 desktop. Chapter 3 shows you how to get help in Windows 98. Chapter 4 is a comprehensive look at files and folders. Chapter 5 covers working with programs and accessories.

The second part of the book shows you how to integrate your computer with the Internet. Chapter 6 shows you how to get connected to the Internet. Chapter 7 covers e-mail and newsgroups. Chapter 8 introduces you to Web browsing, and Chapter 9 explains how to use the new active Web features.

In the third part of the book you will learn some ways to get the most out of your system. Chapter 10 shows you how to customize Windows 98 features to suit your own style and way of working. Chapter 11 shows you some methods for enhancing and maintaining Windows 98 and your computer.

Finally, the appendixes are chock full of useful reference material, including installing Windows 98, troubleshooting, keyboard shortcuts, technical support, and a glossary.

The procedures in the book are written in a clear, step-by-step format. Occasionally you will see a step written like this:

Select Start ➤ Programs ➤ Accessories

This is a shorthand way of saying "Open the Start menu, open the Programs menu that branches from it, then open the Accessories menu that branches from that." When it's appropriate, we use this shorthand method.

You will also find some icons throughout the book that will indicate noteworthy information, useful tips, or handy warnings:

 This icon notes information of special interest.

 This icon calls attention to time-saving hints, features you might miss, or alternative ways of accomplishing tasks.

 This icon alerts you to potential trouble spots, and tells you how to avoid them.

HOW TO USE THE CD-ROM

For installation instructions and how to use the CompuWorks CD-ROM, please refer to Appendix D.

Now let's get started learning Windows 98.

WINDOWS 98 AND YOU

The Windows 98 operating system can bring more power, speed, efficiency and organization to your computer and the work you do with it. With the CompuWorks CD-ROM and Reference Guide, you will be able to take advantage of all that Windows 98 has to offer.

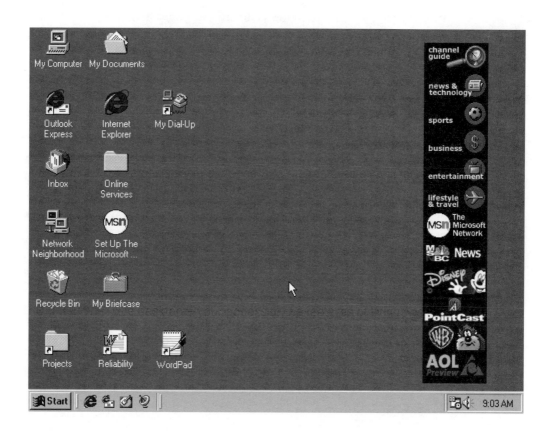

FIGURE 1.1 The desktop—your access to the features of Windows 98

WINDOWS 98 FEATURES

Windows 98 is the latest version of Microsoft Corporation's Windows operating system. Windows 98 maintains the same basic functionality as Windows 95, with a number of significant changes.

The greatest enhancement is in Internet features. Windows comes with a Web browser, Internet Explorer 4.0, and an e-mail program, Outlook Express. Internet features are integrated throughout Windows 98, and so is Internet functionality.

You can access resources on the Web, on your computer, or on a network, in virtually the same way. And you can work with the desktop, and with folders, as if they are Web pages.

Windows 98 is also set up for advanced communications features such as online meeting and TV viewing.

Windows 98 supports MMX processors, and takes advantage of newer hardware technologies including Universal Serial Bus (USB) and Digital Video Disk (DVD).

You will also see more efficient power management, faster programs, better 3D, more ways to personalize Windows, and easier installation of new hardware and software. Windows 98 provides more tools to keep your system running smoothly, including the System File Checker, wizards for troubleshooting and keeping your system tuned up, and the Task Scheduler to coordinate system maintenance.

For now, I'll start with the basics, and then build on that, as I show you how to get the most out of Windows 98.

MIGRATING TO WINDOWS 98

You may be brand new to computers, or you may have some previous experience. Whatever your circumstances, this book and CD-ROM will work for you.

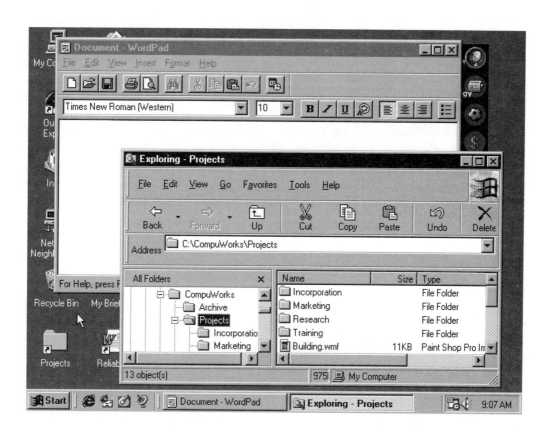

FIGURE 1.2 A folder window and an application window on the desktop

If You Are New to Computers

If Windows 98 is your introduction to computers, use the beginning chapters in this book to build a solid foundation of Windows skills and concepts. Then you can move quickly through the rest of the book, or just through the topics you are interested in.

If You Know Windows 3.1

If you know Windows 3.1, you will already be familiar with many of the basic concepts used in Windows 98 such as icons, folders, and application windows. But there is so much added functionality to Windows 98, not to mention a lot of new features, that we recommend you cover all the information in this book and the accompanying CD-ROM.

If You Know Windows 95

If you know Windows 95, you will find some significant new features in Windows 98. For example, folders can have Web-style functionality, and so can the desktop, which can now include active Web content. Many of the features of Windows 98 work the same way they did in Windows 95, even though they might look a little different. If you are a proficient Windows 95 user, you can move quickly through much of the information in the first part of the book, Chapters 1 through 5.

If You Know the Macintosh

If you are a Macintosh user, then you are already familiar with the concepts of the desktop, windows, files and folders. In general, you should find the adjustment to using Windows 98 a relatively easy one. However, you may want to cover all the information in the book and accompanying CD-ROM to become familiar with the differences in Windows terminology and functionality.

The Windows 98 Desktop

I n this chapter, you'll learn how to use the basic elements of the Windows desktop, including icons, the taskbar, and the Start menu. You will also learn how to work with dialog boxes and windows.

Before you begin (page 6)

The Windows 98 desktop (page 7)

Window basics (page 13)

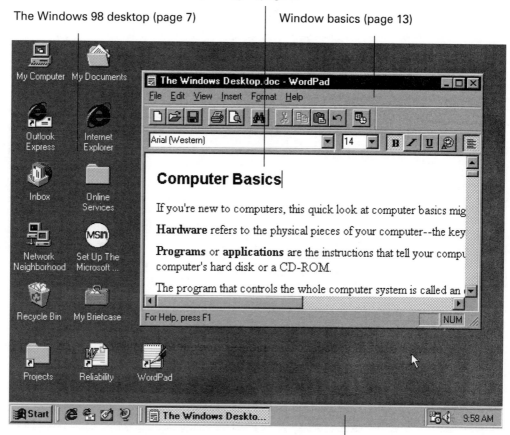

The taskbar (page 9)

FIGURE 2.1 The Windows 98 desktop—your personal computer workspace.

BEFORE YOU BEGIN

Before you begin working with Windows 98, here are some basic computer concepts, and an explanation of how to use the mouse. If you're familiar with these subjects, you can go on to the next section, The Windows Desktop.

Computer Basics

If you're new to computers, this quick look at computer basics might help you understand your system better.

Hardware refers to the physical pieces of your computer—the keyboard, mouse, monitor, modem, and so on.

Programs or **applications** are the instructions that tell your computer what to do. They are stored on a disk, usually the computer's hard disk or a CD-ROM.

The program that controls the whole computer system is called an **operating system**. Windows 98 is an operating system.

Using the Mouse

You can perform many functions in Windows 98 programs by clicking, double-clicking, right-clicking, or dragging with your left and right mouse buttons.

- **Clicking**—Clicking once with the left mouse button selects items on the desktop and in folders.
- **Double-clicking**—Clicking the left mouse button twice in quick succession opens icons.
- **Right-clicking**—Clicking the right mouse button once often brings up a shortcut menu that applies to the surface or program you pointed at.
- **Dragging**—Dragging is a way to move something with the mouse pointer. Point to the item you would like to move, click and *hold* the left mouse button, then slide the mouse pointer across the desktop. When you're done dragging, release the mouse button to drop the item in its new location.

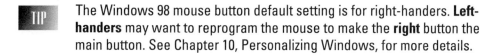

TIP   The Windows 98 mouse button default setting is for right-handers. **Left-handers** may want to reprogram the mouse to make the **right** button the main button. See Chapter 10, Personalizing Windows, for more details.

NOTE   When using Web-style folders, items are selected by pointing and opened by clicking. See Chapter 4, Working with Files and Folders, for more information.

THE WINDOWS 98 DESKTOP
▪▪▪

When you turn on your computer, Windows 98 starts automatically, and the Windows 98 desktop displays (Figure 2.2).

NOTE   If Windows 98 is not installed on your computer, see Appendix A, Installing Windows 98.

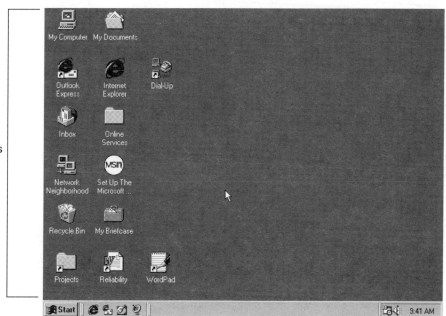

FIGURE 2.2   The Windows 98 desktop

The Windows 98 desktop is your personal computer workspace. The desktop provides quick access to your work, and to the tools you work with. Desktop icons give you an easy way to use what's on your computer. Each icon represents a program, a file, or a location.

 NOTE Don't worry if your desktop doesn't look exactly like the desktop in the figures in this book, or the one on the CompuWorks CD-ROM. The Windows 98 desktop can be customized in different ways. For example, the Channel Bar is not displayed in this book until we need it. For more details see Chapter 10, Personalizing Windows 98.

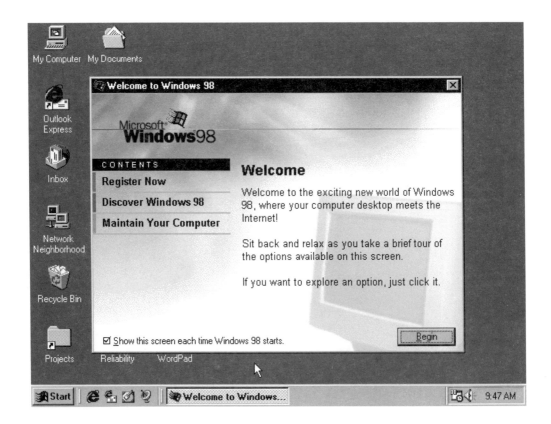

FIGURE 2.3 The Welcome screen

This Welcome screen offers you tips and options to learn more about using Windows 98. It's set to appear whenever Windows starts. To change that, click the *Show this screen each time Windows 98 starts* checkbox to uncheck it. To close the screen, click the X button in the upper right corner of the window (Figure 2.3).

 If you want to use it later, choose Tips and Tour from the Accessories menu (Start ➤ Programs ➤ Accessories ➤ Tips and Tour).

THE TASKBAR

The Windows 98 taskbar includes (Figure 2.4):

Start button: access to programs, documents, and all the features of Windows 98.

Icons: quick access to features, such as the Internet icons in the Quick Launch toolbar.

Buttons: for programs and folders that are open.

Time: displays the time from the internal system clock.

FIGURE 2.4   The Windows 98 taskbar

Using the Start Menu

- To open the Start menu, click the Start button.
- Selecting a menu item followed by a three-dot ellipsis displays a dialog box.
- Pointing to or selecting a menu item with a triangular arrow displays a sub-menu, also called a cascading menu.
- To close this or any other menu or list without making a selection, click outside it (Figure 2.5).

> **NOTE** A **dialog box** is used to give instructions to your computer, when it needs information to complete a task.

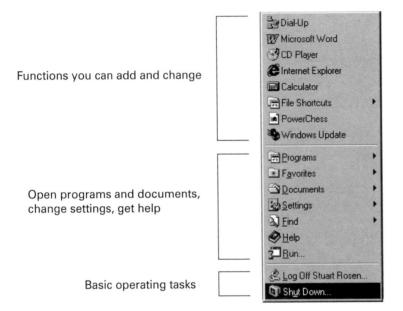

Functions you can add and change

Open programs and documents, change settings, get help

Basic operating tasks

FIGURE 2.5 The Start menu

Resetting the Time and Date

The computer's internal clock is powered by an extended-life battery, so it continues to run when the computer is turned off. Occasionally, though, you may need to reset the time or date. For example, the computer clock might be a little fast or slow. Also, though Windows 98 automatically keeps track of the correct dates in a leap year, you'll need to reset the clock when Daylight Savings Time begins and ends.

To reset the time or date follow these steps:

1 Right-click the time in the taskbar.

2 From the shortcut menu, select **Adjust Date and Time**.

3 In the Date/Time Properties dialog box, set each part of the time by clicking in it, then clicking the small up or down arrows (Figure 2.6).

4 Set the date by selecting it in the calendar.

5 Set the month by clicking the arrow next to the current month, and selecting a month from the drop-down list.

6 Set the year by clicking in it, then using the small arrows.

7 Click OK to save the new settings.

 You may have heard about some computer systems not being able to handle dates for the year 2000 and beyond. This issue is often referred to as Y2K. Windows 98 deals with this issue by interpreting a two-digit year entry as a year between 1930 and 2029.

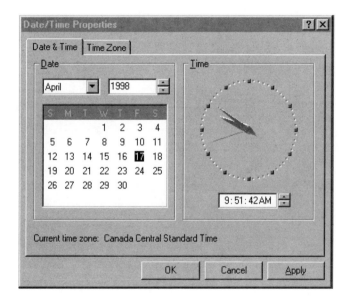

FIGURE 2.6 The Date/Time Properties dialog box

Hiding the Taskbar Clock

You may not need or want the time to display in the taskbar. You can easily hide the taskbar clock.

To hide the clock:

1 Right-click in an empty area of the taskbar.

2 From the shortcut menu, select **Properties**.

3 In the Taskbar Properties dialog box, click the *Show Clock* checkbox to deselect it (Figure 2.7).

FIGURE 2.7 The Taskbar Properties dialog box

4 Click OK. The time no longer displays in the taskbar.

Hiding the Taskbar

To have more room on your desktop, or to make a cleaner-looking desktop, you may want to hide the taskbar. When the taskbar is hidden, you can display it simply by pointing at the bottom of the desktop.

To hide the taskbar:

1   Right-click in an empty area of the taskbar.

2   From the short-cut menu, select **Properties**.

3   In the Taskbar Properties dialog box, click *Auto Hide* to deselect it.

4   Click OK. The taskbar is hidden.

WINDOW BASICS

Most of the work you do on the desktop is done in a window, usually a program window or a folder window. You can see a typical example of a program window by opening WordPad, a Windows 98 word processing accessory (for more details on WordPad see Chapter 5, Running Programs and Accessories).

To open the WordPad window:

1   Click the Start button.

2   On the Start menu, point to Programs.

3   On the Programs submenu, point to Accessories.

4   On the Accessories submenu, click WordPad. The WordPad window opens.

Here is a list of the common elements of a program window (Figure 2.8):

Title bar—shows the title of the document, and the title of the program. To move a window, click and drag its title bar.

Control icon (left end of the title bar)—displays a menu for working with the window.

Minimize button—Minimizes the window to a button on the taskbar. You can also minimize or restore an open window by clicking on its taskbar button.

Maximize button—Maximizes the window to fill the desktop.

Restore button (when the window is maximized)—restores the window to its previous size. To resize a window, drag a side or corner.

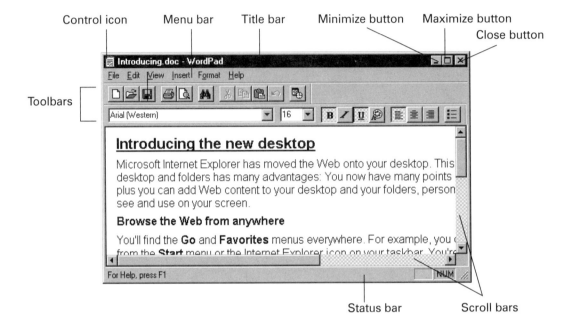

FIGURE 2.8 The WordPad window

Close button—closes the window. You can also close a window by right-clicking its taskbar button, and selecting Close from the shortcut menu.

Menu bar—contains menus that give access to the program's features.

Toolbars—contains buttons that give quick access to program features.

Scroll bars—let you view the entire contents of the window when it is too big to fit on the screen. To scroll a window, click the scroll arrows, or drag the scroll box.

Status bar—contains information about the program and the current file.

Switching Between Windows

You can have many windows open on the desktop at the same time, including programs, folders, or Windows utilities like Help.

There are three ways to switch between windows. You can:

- Click a window,
- Click a window's taskbar button, or
- Hold the Alt key, and press the Tab key until the window you want is displayed.

Arranging Windows on the Desktop

Windows 98 offers a number of options for arranging windows on the desktop. The choices in the taskbar short-cut menu include:

- **Cascade Windows**—overlaps the windows in a cascade arrangement, with all title bars visible.
- **Tile Horizontally**—stacks the windows across the desktop, one above the other.
- **Tile Vertically**—Lines up the windows next to each other, from left to right (Figure 2.9).

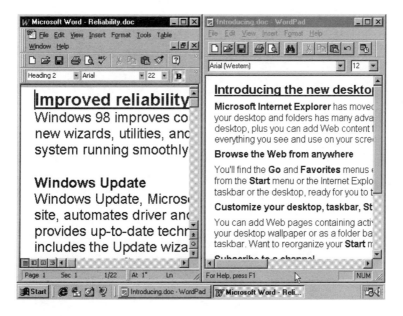

FIGURE 2.9   Windows tiled vertically

Sharing Information Between Programs

Windows 98 makes it easy to share information (text, numbers, graphics, and so on) between programs. You can copy and paste, or cut and paste, from one program to another.

To share information between programs:

1   Select the item you want to move.

2   Right-click it.

3   From the shortcut menu, select **Copy** (or **Cut**).

4   Right-click where the information is to be moved.

5   From the shortcut menu, select **Paste**. The information is moved.

 Between some Windows programs you can cut and paste information by dragging, or copy and paste by holding the Control key and dragging.

GETTING HELP

I n case you're stuck about how to use a certain feature or perplexed about where to find a function you want to work with, Windows 98 comes with an easy-to-use Help feature. Help is available in virtually all programs that run in Windows, and those Help features work similarly to the Windows 98 Help feature.

Finding help with the Help tabs (page 18)   Using additional Help features (page 22)

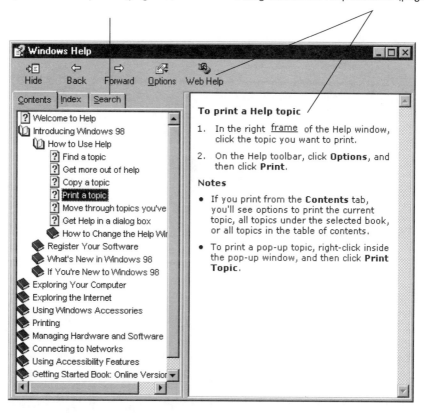

FIGURE 3.1   The Windows 98 Help feature

FINDING HELP WITH THE HELP TABS

To access the Windows 98 Help feature, follow these steps:

1 Open the Start menu.

2 Select Help. The Web-style Help window opens.

You have three choices for finding help (Figure 3.2):

- You can browse through the Help contents,
- You can use the Help index, or
- You can search for words or phrases that might be contained in a Help topic.

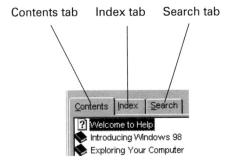

FIGURE 3.2   Help tabs offer different ways to find help.

Using the Help Contents Tab

The Contents tab organizes Help topics into categories and subcategories (Figure 3.3). If you want to learn more about a particular area of Windows 98, or if you want to explore different categories, the Contents tab is the way to do it.

To browse through the Help contents, follow these steps:

1 Select the Contents tab in the left frame of the Help window.

2 Click a category.

3 Click a subcategory.

4 Click a topic. The Help topic you selected displays in the right frame.

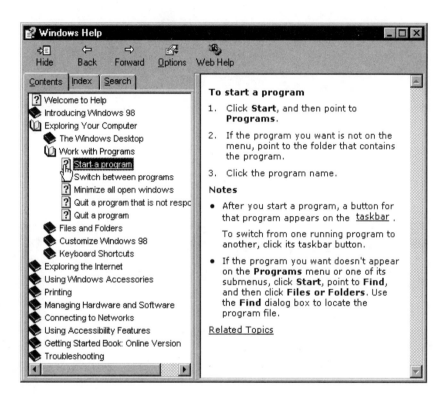

FIGURE 3.3 The Help window, using the Contents tab

Using the Help Index Tab

The Index tab organizes Help topics in an alphabetical list. If you know a particular subject you want help on—a feature, a problem, or a task you want to accomplish—type in a word to go to it in the index (Figure 3.4). You can also simply scroll the index list to display the topic you want.

To use the Help index, follow these steps:

1   Select the Index tab in the Help window.

2   Start typing the subject you're looking for in the text box. As you type the letters, you will notice that the index scrolls to display the best match to what you've typed.

3   When you see the topic you are looking for, double-click it. If it is highlighted, you can simply press Enter. If there's more than one topic for the index listing you select, a dialog box will give you choices of specific Help topics.

The Help topic you selected displays in the right frame.

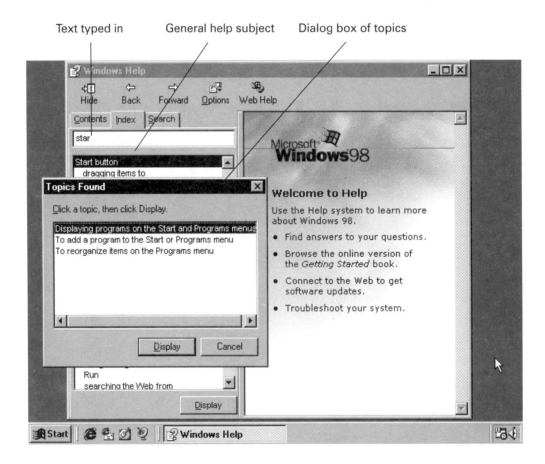

F I G U R E 3.4   The Help window, using the Index tab, with a dialog box of topic choices

Using the Help Search Tab

If you don't know the name of a feature or problem, you can search for the information you want using key words or phrases that might be contained in a Help topic (Figure 3.5).

To search for help, follow these steps:

1 Select the Search tab.

2 Type in a word or phrase in the keyword text box.

3 Click the List Topics button. A list of topics displays.

4 Double-click a topic.

The topic displays in the right frame.

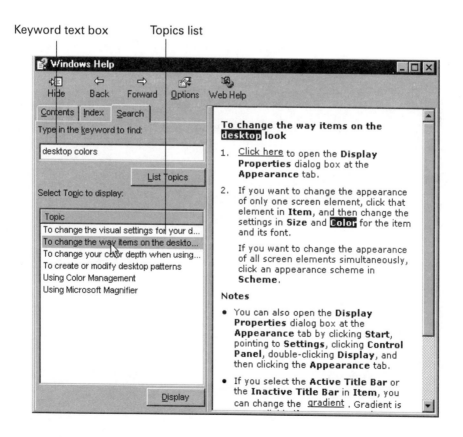

FIGURE 3.5 The Help window, using the Search tab

USING ADDITIONAL HELP FEATURES

Window 98 offers some additional Help features, including underlined help, help buttons, and help by pointing, that enable you to get the help you need quickly and easily.

Understanding Underlined Help Features

When you display Help topics in the right pane, you'll notice that they often contain underlined words and phrases. Clicking these underlined items can give you additional help (Figure 3.6):

- Clicking a term that is underlined displays a pop-up window that explains the meaning of the term.
- Clicking a term that is underlined and colored triggers an action, such as opening a program or displaying another Help topic.
- Clicking the underlined phrase *related topics* displays more help topics related to the current topic.

Using Help Buttons

The buttons in the Help toolbar give you more ways to work with Help topics. Here is a list of what you can achieve by clicking the individual buttons:

Hide—hides the left frame, so you can see more of your desktop

Back—moves back through Help topics you've displayed.

Forward—moves forward through Help topics you've displayed.

Options—includes an option to print Help topics.

Web Help—connects you to online Web help from Microsoft.

Pointing to Get Help

You can often get a quick explanation of something in Windows 98 by pointing to it.

For example:

- Pointing at an icon often displays a pop-up box that describes it. (The icon might need to be selected.)

Colored underlined term, for action   Underlined term, for pop-up explanation

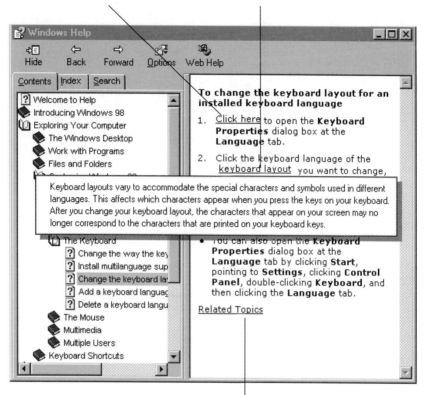

FIGURE 3.6   Underlined words and phrases in a Help topic

- Pointing at a toolbar button displays a pop-up description called a tool-tip.

- Pointing at a program button in the taskbar displays the name of the program and the name of the current document.

- Pointing at a menu item in a folder window often displays text that describes it at the left end of the status bar (Figure 3.7).

As you work with Window 98, you'll find other instances where pointing to an item or feature displays helpful information about it.

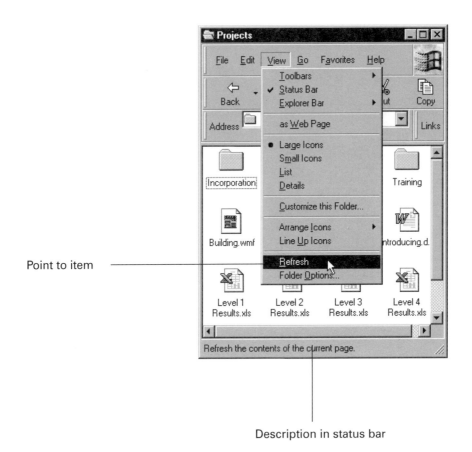

Point to item

Description in status bar

FIGURE 3.7 The status bar lists a brief description of the menu item

WORKING WITH FILES AND FOLDERS

4

The documents that you create, such as letters, spreadsheets, graphics, and so on, are each stored as a file. The instructions that run programs are also stored as files, and files are arranged in folders. Windows 98 makes it easy to organize and work with your files and folders. This chapter covers file and folder basics, file management, and folder display options.

Managing files with Windows Explorer (page 30)   File and folder basics (page 26)

Changing folder views (page 37)

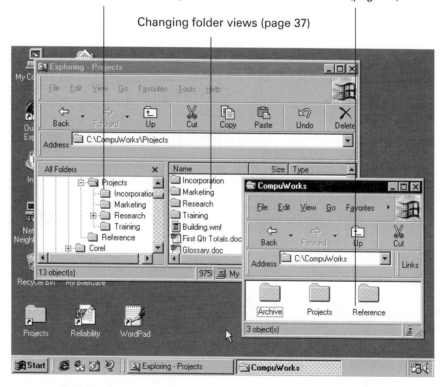

FIGURE 4.1   Get ready to work with files and folders.

FILE AND FOLDER BASICS
▪▪

When you are working with files and folders, you want to be able to create new folders, rename folders, and view your disk drives with the My Computer folder.

Viewing the Contents of a Folder

The folder window in Figure 4-2 contains icons for folders and document files. To view the contents of a folder, double-click the folder icon.

Double-click folder icon
to view folder contents

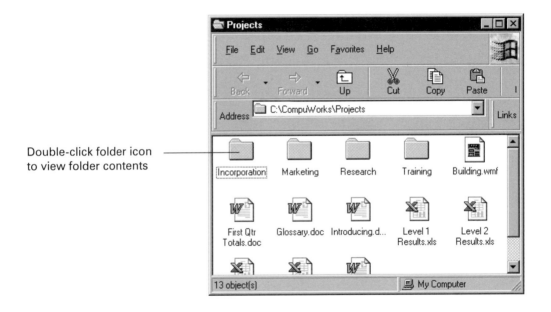

FIGURE 4.2   A folder window with icons for folders and files

 You can work with the files and folders on your computer to practice using these Windows 98 features. We recommend that you use folders that contain your documents, rather than folders that contain files that run your programs. Copying, moving, or deleting program files causes problems in running those programs.

Creating a New Folder

To create a new folder, follow these easy steps:

1   Make sure a folder window is open.

2   Open the File menu.

3   Point to New. (If the "New" choice doesn't display in the File menu, click in the folder Address line, then open the File menu again.)

4   From the submenu, select **Folder**. The new folder appears, with a default name and the name is selected as shown as follows:

5   Type a new name for the folder.

6   Press Enter.

The new folder is created and named.

Renaming a File or Folder

To rename a file or folder, follow these easy steps:

1   Select the file or folder icon by clicking it once.

2   Click the icon name to select it.

3   Type the new name if you want to rename the file or folder.

 If you only want to edit an existing name, click in the name again to position the cursor. Then add and delete the text you want.

4   Press Enter.

The folder is renamed.

What's in a Name?

Files and folders use the same naming rules. A name can contain up to 255 characters, as well as spaces. However, it cannot contain any of these characters:

\ / : * ? " < > |

In addition, file names cab have an extension of up to 3 characters, separated from the name by a period (for example, *First Qtr Totals.doc*). The extension usually indicates what kind of file it is.

The extensions are usually assigned by a program when you create a file, and tell Windows with what program the file should be opened. For example, the *.doc* extension is used for Microsoft Word files. Double-clicking a filename with that extension will launch Microsoft Word, and then open the file.

Displaying File Extensions

Windows includes an option to show or hide the extensions of file types that it recognizes. If your folder windows display files with their extensions hidden, you can show them easily.

To display all file extensions:

1   Open the View menu in the menu bar.

2   Select **Folder Options**.

3   In the Folder Options dialog box, make sure the View tab is selected.

4   In the Advanced Settings list, make sure that *Hide file extensions for known file types* is not checked (Figure 4.3).

5   Select OK.

All file extensions will now display.

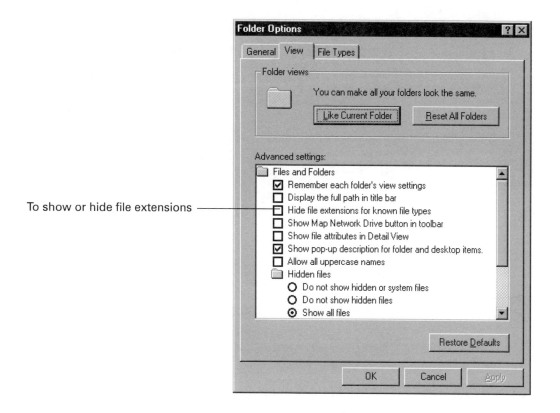

To show or hide file extensions ——————

FIGURE 4.3   The Folder Options dialog box, with the View tab selected

Using the My Computer Folder

The My Computer folder enables you to easily get at all the files on your computer (Figure 4.4):

1   Double-click the My Computer icon on the desktop.

2   Double-click any drive to view its contents.

This folder shows all the disk drives on your computer. You can work with the My Computer window just as you would with any other folder window.

 With the exception of Windows Explorer, opening a folder displays the contents in a new folder window. To change this, open the Folder Options dialog box from the View menu, select Custom Settings on the General tab, and set it to browse folders by opening each one of them in the same window.

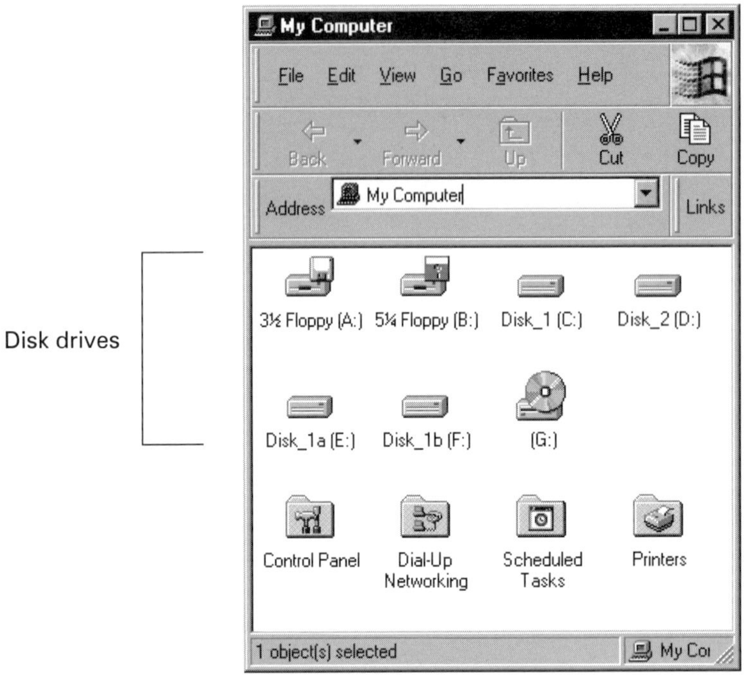

Disk drives

FIGURE 4.4   The My Computer folder window

MANAGING FILES WITH WINDOWS EXPLORER

Windows Explorer displays more features than other folder windows, and I'll use it for the remainder of this chapter. However, many of the functions we cover with Windows Explorer—such as moving or deleting files—can also be done in other folder windows.

> **NOTE**   Windows 98 also provides keyboard shortcuts for moving, copying, and deleting files. See Appendix C, Keyboard Shortcuts, for the details.

Viewing Files and Folders with Windows Explorer

To open Windows Explorer, follow these simple steps:

1 From the Start Menu, select Programs.

2 Select Windows Explorer from the Programs menu.

3 Resize or maximize the Windows Explorer window so all the toolbar buttons display.

NOTE If you are unfamiliar with resizing and maximizing a window, see the Windows Basics section of Chapter 2, The Windows Desktop.

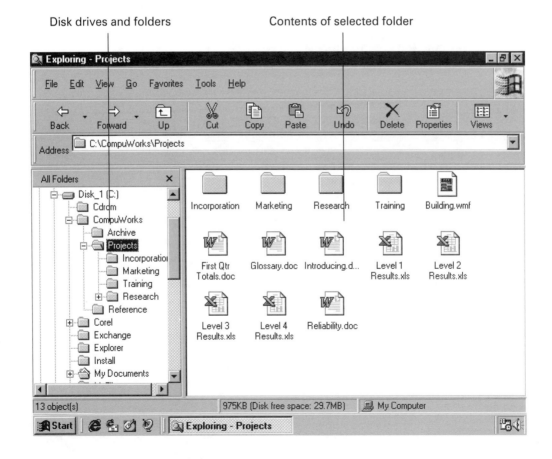

F I G U R E 4.5 The Windows Explorer window

Windows Explorer makes it easy to find and display folders and their contents (Figure 4.5).

The **left pane** shows all disk drives and folders. Here's how to navigate this part of Windows Explorer:

- Clicking a folder in the left pane displays its contents in the right pane.
- Clicking a plus sign shows that folder's subfolders in the left pane.
- Clicking a minus sign hides subfolders.

The **right pane** shows the contents of the selected folder.

The buttons in the **toolbar** provide quick access to some powerful features:

Back moves you backwards through the displayed folders.

Forward moves you forwards through the displayed folders.

Up moves you up through levels of folders.

Cut cuts a selection, storing it temporarily in the Clipboard (see note below).

Copy copies a selection, storing it temporarily in the Clipboard.

Paste pastes Clipboard contents to the current location.

Undo reverses the editing action (for example, cutting or pasting) or cancels the previous step.

Delete sends the selected file or folder and its contents to the Recycle Bin.

Properties displays the properties of the selected item. Properties include the item type, location, size, and when it was created.

Views changes the way items are displayed in the window. (See the section, Changing Folder Views, later in this chapter.)

NOTE The Windows Clipboard is a section of the computer's memory that holds items, usually temporarily, that you cut or copy from one location to paste to another location. The Clipboard can hold virtually anything—folders, files, graphics, text, and so on.

Moving a File or Folder

You can move an icon to a folder icon, to a folder window, or to the desktop. There are a variety of ways to move file and folder icons. You can move a file or folder by:

- dragging,
- cutting and pasting using the toolbar, or by
- cutting and pasting using menus.

To move a file by **dragging**, follow these steps:

1   Make sure the icon you want to move is displayed.

2   Make sure the location to which you want to move it is displayed.

3   Drag the icon to its new location, and drop it there.

 Dragging is a way to move something with the mouse pointer. Point to the item you would like to move, click and *hold* the left mouse button, then slide the mouse pointer across the desktop. When you're done dragging, release the mouse button to drop the item in its new location.

Here are some exceptions to moving files and folders by dragging:

- If you drag an icon to another **disk drive**, the icon is automatically copied. To move an icon to another disk drive, hold the **Shift** key while you drag it.

- If you drag an *.exe* file—a file that runs a program—to another location, Windows will create a shortcut for it instead of moving it. **To move an *.exe* file**, use Cut and Paste. To learn more about creating shortcuts, see Chapter 10, Personalizing Windows 98.

To move a file by **cutting and pasting using the toolbar**, follow these steps:

1   Select the icon you want to move.

2   Click the Cut button on the toolbar.

3   Make sure the location to which you want to move the icon is displayed.

4   Click that location.

5   Click the Paste button in the toolbar.

To move a file by **cutting and pasting using menus**, follow these steps:

1 Right-click the icon you want to move (Figure 4.6).

2 From the shortcut menu, select **Cut**.

3 Make sure the location to which you want to move the icon is displayed.

4 Right-click that location.

5 From the shortcut menu, select **Paste**.

FIGURE 4.6 The icon shortcut menu

 The Edit menu in the menu bar also includes the Cut, Copy, and Paste choices.

Copying a File or Folder

Copying files and folders with Windows 98 is similar to moving them. Here are the differences:

- If you want to copy a file or folder by dragging, hold the Control key while you drag and drop the icon.

- If you want to copy by dragging to another disk drive, drag without holding any keys.

- If you drag an *.exe* file—a file that runs a program—to another location, Windows will create a shortcut for it instead of copying it. **To copy an *.exe* file**, use Copy and Paste. To learn more about creating shortcuts, see Chapter 10, Personalizing Windows 98.

- If you want to copy a file or folder by copying and pasting, use the Copy button on the toolbar, or the Copy choice on the shortcut or Edit menus.

Selecting Multiple Items

Sometimes you want to work with a number of items all at once. Once you've selected multiple items, you can move, copy, or delete them just as you would single items.

To select multiple items, you should:

1   Press and hold the Control key.

2   Select each item.

To deselect an item, you should:

1   Press and hold the Control key.

2   Select the item again.

To select multiple contiguous items, you should:

1   Select the first item.

2   Hold the Shift key.

3   Select the last item in the contiguous group.

To deselect all selected items, you should:

1   Release any keys.

2   Click outside of the selection.

Deleting Files or Folders

Reclaim valuable hard disk space by deleting files and folders you no longer need. You can delete files and folders by:

- dragging them to the Recycle Bin,
- using the toolbar, or
- using a menu.

To delete a file or folder by dragging it to the Recycle Bin, follow these steps:

1 Make sure the icon you want to delete is displayed.

2 Make sure the Recycle Bin is displayed on the desktop, or in the left pane of Windows Explorer.

3 Drag the icon to the Recycle Bin, and drop it there. The "Are you sure?" dialog box appears.

4 Click Yes.

To delete a file or folder by using the toolbar, follow these steps:

1 Select the icon you want to delete.

2 Click the Delete button in the toolbar.

3 In the "Are you sure?" dialog box, click Yes.

To delete a file or folder by using a menu, follow these steps:

1 Right-click the icon you want to delete.

2 From the shortcut menu, select **Delete**.

3 In the "Are you sure?" dialog box, click Yes.

 The File menu in the menu bar also includes a Delete choice.

Retrieving Deleted Files

If you accidentally delete a file or folder, you can still retrieve it. The Recycle Bin is a folder where deleted items are held temporarily, until you empty it.

 Items deleted from your hard drive go to the Recycle Bin. Items deleted from a floppy disk are permanently deleted.

To access the Recycle Bin:

1 Double-click the Recycle Bin folder to open it.

2 Select the file(s) or folder(s) you want to undelete.

3 Select **Restore** from the File menu.

4 Your files will be moved to the location from which they were originally deleted.

NOTE You can also move the files and folders you want to retrieve to another location by dragging or cutting and pasting.

TIP To permanently delete a hard disk item without sending it to the Recycle Bin, hold the Shift key during the delete process.

To undo the *last* deletion you made, just click the Undo button in the toolbar, or select Undo Delete from the Edit menu.

Emptying the Recycle Bin

Eventually, even the Recycle Bin will fill up. When this happens, Windows automatically deletes the oldest items to make room for the newer ones. It's a good idea to empty what you want from the Recycle Bin, when you want to. Emptying the Recycle Bin is also a good way to free up space on your hard drive.

To empty the Recycle Bin:

1 Move items you want to save out of the Recycle Bin.

2 Right-click the Recycle Bin icon.

3 In the shortcut menu, select **Empty Recycle Bin**.

4 In the "Are you sure?" dialog box, click Yes.

CHANGING FOLDER VIEWS

With Windows 98, you can change how folder icons display and how they're sorted. You can even give your folders Web-style functionality, and view them as Web pages.

Changing the Appearance of Icons

The Views button on the folder window toolbar enables you to change how you view icons. You can choose large or small icons, listed icons, or icons with details of file type, size, and modification date and time.

To change the appearance of icons:

1 Click on the Views button dropdown arrow.

2 Select the view you want from the list (Figure 4.7).

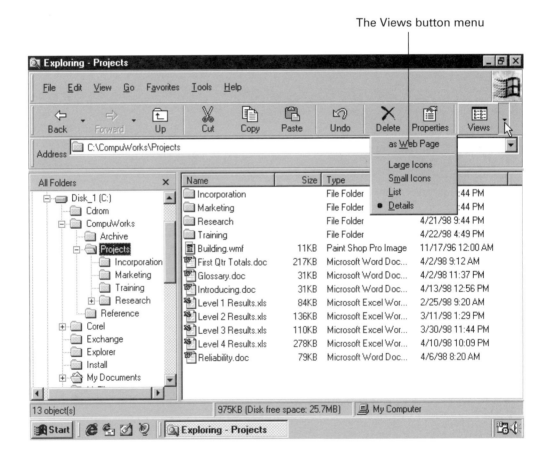

The Views button menu

FIGURE 4.7 Folder contents in Detail view

You can also cycle through each view choice by repeatedly clicking the Views button.

Changing How Icons Are Sorted

In the Details view, you can sort items by each of the categories displayed:

- Clicking a column header sorts items by that category, in ascending order.
- Clicking the header a second time sorts items in descending order.

The View menu in the menu bar offers these same choices. If you sort with the View menu choices, you can also be in the Large Icons, Small Icons, or List view.

Using Web-Style Functionality

The standard folder functionality is the "classic" Windows 95 style—selecting an item by clicking, opening it by double-clicking. In Windows 98, you can also display folder windows so they have Web-style functionality—pointing to an item selects it, and clicking opens it.

To take advantage of this new feature, follow these steps:

1 Open the View menu in the menu bar.

2 Select **Folder Options**.

3 In the Folder Options dialog box, make sure the General tab is selected.

4 Select **Web-style**.

5 Select OK.

Items now display underlined, and have Web-style functionality.

When Folders have Web-style functionality, the desktop automatically does also, and displays as a Web page, with the Channel bar. To learn more about the Web-style desktop, see Chapter 9, Using Active Web Features.

 You can customize this look and functionality in the Folder Options dialog box.

Viewing Folders as Web Pages

Not only can you give folders Web-style functionality, you can also view them as Web pages (Figure 4.8). Here's what you need to do:

1 Open the View menu in the menu bar.

2 Select **As Web Page**.

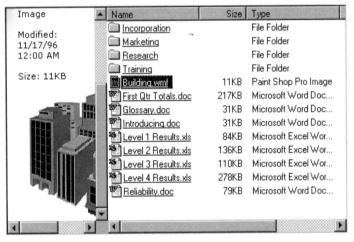

FIGURE 4.8 Web-style folder window in Web view

The right pane displays as a Web page, and a middle pane shows information about the selected item. The middle right pane can preview some files, such as graphic files. Selecting a disk drive icon displays a pie chart showing disk space usage.

5

RUNNING PROGRAMS
AND ACCESSORIES

· ·

One of the benefits of the Windows operating system is that application programs and accessories created to run in Windows have a lot of similarities in the way they are used. Many of the features are the same, whether you are using a word processor, a spreadsheet, a graphics program, or any other type of program. You will find these program similarities no matter what company created the program. In this chapter, you'll learn how to work with Windows programs and use the Windows 98 accessories.

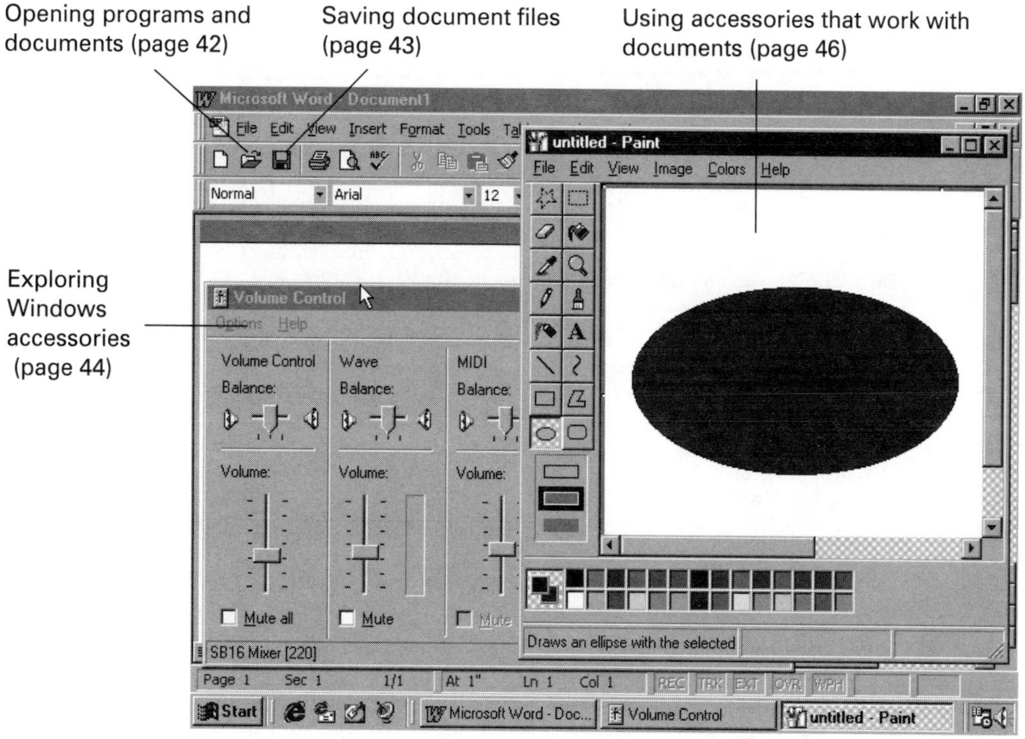

Opening programs and documents (page 42)

Saving document files (page 43)

Using accessories that work with documents (page 46)

Exploring Windows accessories (page 44)

FIGURE 5.1 You can choose from many programs and accessories

OPENING PROGRAMS AND DOCUMENTS

Here are a couple of tasks you'll do quite often—opening a program, and opening a document file in the program.

There are a variety of ways to open a program:

- From the Start menu, select the program from the Programs submenu.
- From the desktop, open the program shortcut icon. (To learn how to add a program to the Start menu, and how to create a shortcut, see Chapter 10, Personalizing Windows 98.)
- From a folder window, open the file that starts the program.
- From the Start menu, select the Run command. Then type in the name of the file that starts the program, or browse your folders to find that file.

 The file that starts a program is a file with the *.exe* extension (short for executable file). The file name usually is the name of the program, sometimes abbreviated, and the file icon is usually the main icon for the program.

A file that you create in a progam—whether it's a letter, a Web page, a graphic, a spreadsheet, and so on, is referred to as a "document."

To open a document file, follow these steps:

1 Make sure a program is open.

2 Click the Open button in the toolbar (or open the File menu and select Open). The Open dialog box displays (Figure 5.2). It's similar to a folder window.

3 If necessary, move through folders and subfolders to find the file you want.

4 Double-click the file (or select it, and click the Open button).

The file opens in the program window.

Open button   Save button

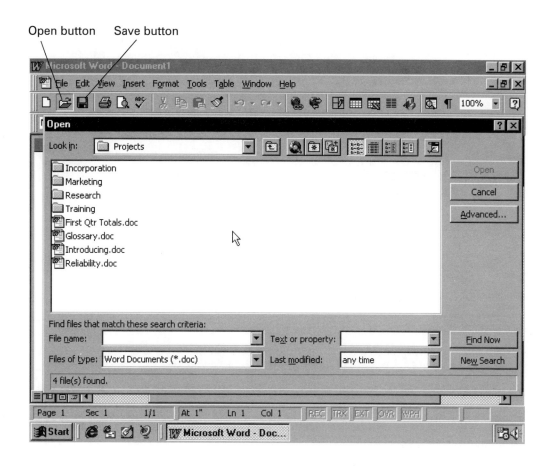

FIGURE 5.2   A program window, with the Open dialog box

SAVING DOCUMENT FILES

Once you've modified an existing file, or created a new one, you want to save it on a disk. Until your work is saved, it only exists in the computer's memory. When the computer is turned off, any unsaved work in the computer's memory will be lost.

To save a file, follow these steps:

1 Click the Save button in the toolbar (or open the File menu and select Save). If you are saving an existing file, the file is now saved and you are done. If you are saving a new file, the Save As dialog box displays. It's similar to the Open dialog box.

2 Make sure the folder in which you want to save the file is displayed. If necessary, move through folders and subfolders to find the location you want.

3 Type in a name in the file name text box.

4 Click OK (or press Enter).

The file is saved.

 In most programs, you can save a file under a new name with the Save As command in the File menu.

EXPLORING WINDOWS ACCESSORIES

Windows 98 comes with a variety of accessory programs that perform many useful tasks, and also provide some entertainment.

Starting Accessories

Windows 98 Accessories are conveniently organized, and easily accessible from the Start menu.

To access the Accessories, you have to:

1 Open the Start menu.

2 Open the Programs submenu.

3 Open the Accessories submenu (Figure 5.3).

 Your Accessory groups and items may be slightly different. To learn more about adding accessories, see Chapter 11, Enhancing and Maintaining Your System.

FIGURE 5.3 The Accessories submenu

Working with Accessory Groups

Here is a list of the standard Accessory groups, and some of their features:

- **Communications**—This group contains features that enable you to make phone and modem connections, as well as direct cable connections to other computers. HyperTerminal enables modem-to-modem connections with another computer.

- **Entertainment**—This group contains features that enable you to control and play audio and video. CD Player enables you to play music CDs through your computer. Volume Control enables you to control the volume and balance of audio playing on your computer.

- **Games**—This group contains a number of classic Windows games—just for fun

- **System Tools**—This group contains features that enable you to maintain and optimize your system. Backup enables you to back up selected files to a separate disk or a tape—for your safety. Scheduled Tasks is for scheduling automatic system maintenance.

 We'll explain these and other system tools in Chapter 11, Enhancing and Maintaining Your System.

Controlling Volume and Balance

The speaker icon in the taskbar gives you quick access to volume control. You can:

- Right-click the speaker icon and select Open Volume Controls to display the full volume control dialog box (Figure 5.4, left), or
- Click the speaker icon to display a basic volume and mute control (Figure 5.4, right).

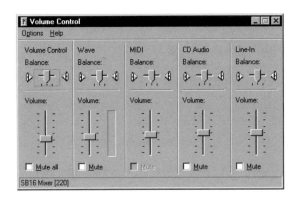 

FIGURE 5.4   The Volume Control dialog box (left) and the taskbar volume control

The Volume Control dialog box gives you three control options:

- To control balance, drag the balance slider left or right.
- To control volume, drag the volume slider up or down.
- To mute volume, click the *Mute* checkbox.

USING ACCESSORIES APPLICATIONS
∎∎∎

Some Accessories enable you to view, create, and edit documents, including

- **Notepad**, which is often used to create, read, and edit ASCII (plain text) files.
- **WordPad**, which is a basic word processor that enables you to create, edit, and view documents. WordPad files can be worked with in Microsoft Word, and vice versa.

- **Imaging**, which enables you to view and perform basic tasks on image documents, such as scanned images and faxes.
- **Paint**, which is a program with which you can create graphics.

Opening a Document in Notepad

The Notepad accessory is a simple text editor that works with ASCII text, which is plain text not specific to any particular word processor. ASCII text files are just text, without any formatting, and usually have a *.txt* file extension.

To open a text file in Notepad you can open Notepad, and then use the File menu to open the file. It's often easier just to open a *.txt* file by double-clicking it in a folder window, and Windows will automatically open it in Notepad.

Many programs come with text files that contain information about the program. Notepad provides a handy way to read these files. Windows 98 includes some informational text files, including one in the Online Services folder.

To open the Online Services text file in Notepad, follow these steps:

1 In Windows Explorer, open the Online Services folder

2 Double-click the *About Online Services.txt* icon. The file opens in Notepad (Figure 5.5).

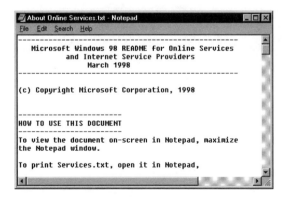

FIGURE 5.5 The Notepad window with the About Online Services file

You can use the scroll bars to view the file, which contains information about connecting to Internet services. While you wouldn't edit a file like this one, you can do basic text editing with Notepad.

Creating a Document with WordPad

The WordPad accessory is a simple word processor. You can use it to create and edit documents, with basic formatting such as boldfacing, italicizing, and underlining, and alignment choices such as centering.

To create a document in WordPad with a bold, centered heading, you should:

1   Select Start ➤ Programs ➤ Accessories.

2   Select WordPad. The WordPad window opens.

3   Click the Bold button.

4   Type: The Story of [your name]

5   Press Enter to end the line.

6   Press Enter again to add a blank line.

7   Click the Align Left button to move the cursor to the left margin.

You could continue to type and edit the document, saving your work with the Save button. One of the helpful features of WordPad is that its files can be read by Microsoft Word, and vice versa (Figure 5.6).

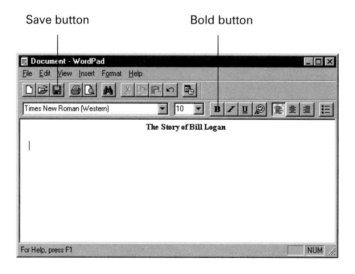

FIGURE 5.6   A WordPad document with a bold heading

Viewing a Document with Kodak Imaging

If you want a quick way to view just about any graphic file, scanned image, or even a fax you've received through your computer, the Imaging accessory from Kodak can be a very helpful tool.

To view a document with Imaging, follow these steps:

1   Select Start ➤ Programs ➤ Accessories.

2   Select Imaging. The Imaging program opens.

3   Click the Open button. The Open dialog box displays.

4   Make sure that *All Image Files* is selected in the Files of Type line.

5   Open the Windows folder.

6   Select the *Setup.bmp* file (near the end of the icons in the folder). The Windows Setup graphic displays (Figure 5.7).

You can change the image view in a variety of ways. You can:

- Fit the image in the window with the Best Fit button.
- Zoom in and out with the Zoom buttons.
- Rotate the image with the Rotate buttons.

If you save a file used by a program, such as the Windows 98 *Setup.bmp* file, be sure to save it with a new name, so the original file will remain unchanged.

Creating a Graphic with the Paint Program

The Paint accessory enables you to easily create graphics that you can print out, or add to other documents (Figure 5.8).

To create a graphic with the Paint program, follow these steps:

1   Select a tool from the Tool box.

2   Choose a setting for width, border, fill, and so on, below the Tool box.

3   Select color(s) from the Color box. For shapes, select border color with the left mouse button, and fill color with the right mouse button.

4   Drag the mouse in the drawing area to create the graphic. You can continue to add graphic elements in this way. Save the graphic with the Save command in the File menu. (You can undo the last thing you did with the Undo command from the Edit menu. Pressing Control+Z also runs the Undo command.)

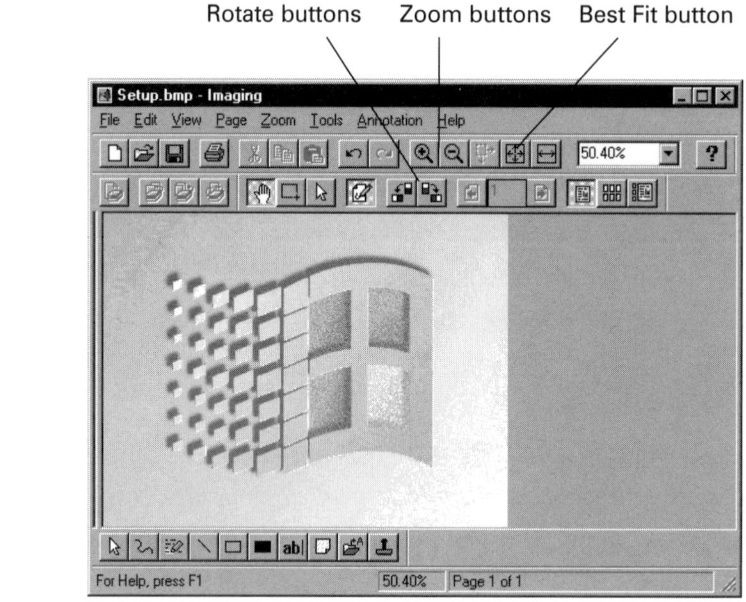

Rotate buttons   Zoom buttons   Best Fit button

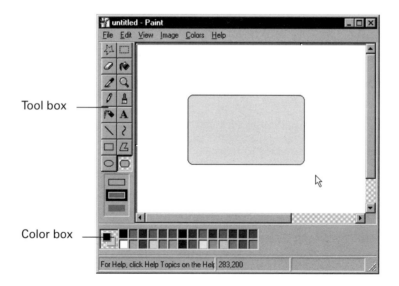

FIGURE 5.7   Viewing a graphic file in Imagiing

FIGURE 5.8   The Paint accessory

6

INTEGRATING THE INTERNET

$\mathbf{I}$f you have a computer, sooner or later you'll want to connect to the Internet. In this chapter you'll learn basic Internet concepts, what you need to connect to the Internet, and how to set up an Internet connection.

The Internet (page 52)

Setting up an Internet connection (page 55)

Getting ready for Internet access (page 52)

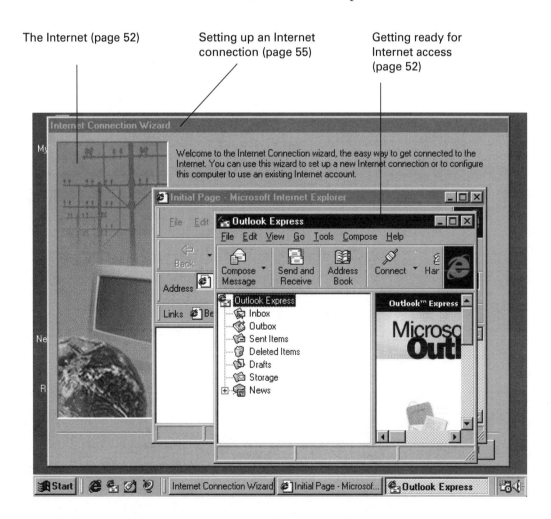

FIGURE 6.1 Connect to the Internet and the World Wide Web

THE INTERNET

The Internet is a network of connected computers, all around the world. It enables people to find and share information between all those interconnected computers. With an Internet connection, you can send and receive e-mail, read and post messages to newsgroups, and browse the World Wide Web.

A Little Internet History

In recent years, the Internet has generated incredible interest from the computer industry and the general public. But the Internet is not a new concept. The military developed it in the 1960s, as a communications network designed to survive a nuclear attack. In the 1970s, scientists and academics began using e-mail as a way to communicate with each other. Internet use continued to grow throughout the 1980s, mainly in academic circles.

The World Wide Web

By 1990 an Internet service called the World Wide Web was developed. Web pages are documents that can contain text, graphics, animation, audio, and video. Web pages are interconnected by "hyperlinks," text or graphics that link to other Web pages. When you click on a link, that page is displayed.

GETTING READY FOR INTERNET ACCESS

The procedures in this section will help you get ready for Internet access.

To connect to the Internet, you'll need:

- Hardware
- Software
- An Internet service provider (ISP)

Hardware

If you're already connected to a local area network (LAN) your hardware is ready. You may be connected to a network through the company you work for.

If, like most home computers, your computer is not on a network, you will need a modem, a device that enables your computer to send and receive data over a phone line. Most new computers come with modems already installed. Your modem needs to be connected to a phone line.

Software

You need a Web browser and an e-mail program. Windows 98 comes with Internet Explorer for browsing the Web, and Outlook Express for sending and receiving e-mail and participating in newsgroups. (Most e-mail programs work with news-groups as well.)

There are lots of other Internet programs available that you can get and install on your computer, but to take full advantage of the Windows 98 Internet features, such as Channels and the Active Desktop, you'll need to use the Internet programs that come with Windows 98.

Internet Service Provider

An Internet Service Provider (ISP) is a company that provides connections to the Internet, and to servers (large storage computers) for using e-mail and newsgroups. It can be a small local operation or a large company with millions of users.

An ISP is connected directly to the Internet, or is connected to a network that is connected to the Internet. When you set up an account with an ISP, usually for a monthly fee, then you can connect to the Internet through the ISP.

If you've already been connected to the Internet from your computer, or if you're part of a local area network with Internet service, then you already have an ISP connection. You're ready to use the Internet Connection Wizard to set it up for Windows 98 (see the Using the Internet Connection Wizard section below).

If you don't have an ISP, you need to set up an account with an ISP of your choice. You can:

- Choose from the online services provided in Windows 98.
- Choose from a list of ISPs available in your area, provided by Microsoft.
- Find an ISP on your own.

To choose an ISP from the online services provided in Windows 98, follow these steps:

1 Open the Online Services folder on the desktop. In the window, you can open the "About Online Services" file to learn more about this option (Figure 6.2).

2 Open the icon for the online service you're interested in.

3 Follow the instructions. (You'll probably need your Windows 98 installation CD-ROM.)

Once this process is completed, your connection will be set up. You won't need the procedures in the rest of this chapter.

FIGURE 6.2   The Online Services window

To choose an ISP from Microsoft's ISP list, go to the Using the Internet Connection Wizard section.

To find an ISP on your own, you can:

- Ask a friend or colleague for a recommendation. Find out about their experiences with the ISP and the quality of service they have received. Getting a recommendation from someone you trust can be extremely helpful in making a good choice.

- Look up ISPs in the Yellow Pages, under "Internet Products and Services."

- Look for ads in the newspaper, computer magazines, and so on.

Then call the ISP and set up the account. Once you're signed up with an ISP, take down all the information you'll need from them for an Internet connection and a connection to the e-mail server, including:

User name

Password

Domain name

Primary DNS

Secondary DNS

POP server name (for receiving e-mail)

SMPT server name (for sending mail)

NNTP server name (for news groups)

E-mail name

Dial-in number

Tech support number

You are now ready to use the Internet Connection Wizard.

SETTING UP AN INTERNET CONNECTION

Once you have your hardware and software ready, and an ISP, you're ready to set up an Internet connection.

Questions to Ask Your ISP Rep

Here are some questions to ask an ISP representative before you sign up with him or her:

- How long have they been in business? (This tells you how experienced/popular they are.)

- What is the monthly fee?

- Is there a flat rate for unlimited access? If not, how many hours does the fee cover? How much is it for hours over that amount?

- Is there a time limit you can spend online at any time?

- Are there any "one-time" setup charges?

- Is there a local point of presence? Is it a toll or a toll-free call?

- When you travel, can you connect through a local call from your new location?

- Can you get technical support? If so, what hours of the day and days of the week can you call tech support?

- Does the service "max out"? Does the ISP have enough modems for peak loads?

- How many subscribers does the ISP have?

- Are there any storage or download limits?

- Does the ISP give you all the software you need to access it and the Web?

- Do you get free Web publishing space with your monthly fee? Many ISPs offer you server space for your own web site as part of their monthly fee. You may be charged for domain name registration and the amount of traffic your web site generates. Be sure to understand any surcharges that might accrue.

Using the Internet Connection Wizard

Windows 98 offers many wizards or programs that guide you through a particular process.

To access the Internet Connection Wizard, do the following:

1 From the Start menu, open the Programs submenu.

2 From the Internet Explorer submenu, select Connection Wizard.

The Wizard dialog box appears (Figure 6.3).

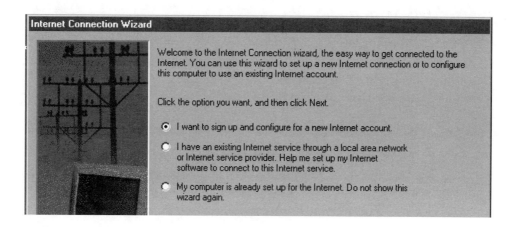

FIGURE 6.3   The Internet Connection Wizard

With this wizard, you can:

- Choose an ISP from a list of ISPs in your area, provided by Microsoft,
- Set up your system for an existing account, or
- Tell the wizard that you already are set up for Internet access and it should not bother you again.

Microsoft can send you a list of ISPs available in your area. You'll connect online via an 800 number, and Microsoft will download the list to your computer.

To choose an ISP from a list of local ISPs provided by Microsoft, follow these steps:

1   Make sure the first Connection Wizard choice is selected.

2   Click the Next button.

Follow the instructions for connecting online to the Microsoft Referral Service.

If you already have an existing account for Internet access, do the following:

1   Select the second Connection Wizard choice from the top.

2   Click the Next button.

Follow the instructions for setting up the connection.

Using Dial-Up Networking

Unless you're on a network, you'll have a dial-up connection set up that you'll use to connect to the Internet. You may have a dial-up icon on the desktop, and you can always find it in the Communications submenu.

To use Dial-Up Networking:

1 Open the Start menu, and the Programs submenu.

2 Open the Accessories menu, and the Communications submenu.

3 Select Dial-Up Networking.

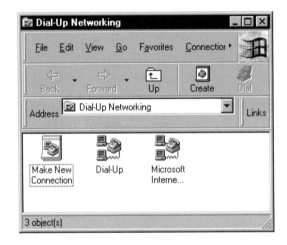

FIGURE 6.4 The Dial-Up Networking folder

The folder displays dial-up icons, along with an icon to make a new connection. When you want to connect to the Internet, open your dial-up connection (Figure 6.4).

You can use virtually any Web browser or e-mail program with your dial-up connection.

 You may find it convenient to have a dial-up icon on the desktop. Icons on the desktop or in folders that open features located elsewhere are called shortcuts. To learn about creating shortcuts, see Chapter 10, Personalizing Windows 98.

Dealing with Connection Problems

No ISP can give you perfect connections whenever you want. The Internet is not a perfect system. From time to time you'll have problems: you'll get a busy signal, you'll get a very slow connection, you'll get disconnected from the ISP's server, or you won't be able to access your e-mail.

Here are some ways to deal with those problems. (None of these are guaranteed fixes, but they'll sometimes help.)

- If you get a busy signal, try again right away. If you continue to get busy signals, make a few more attempts right away. If this doesn't work, wait awhile and try again.

- Busy signals are more likely during peak hours of day. Find out when the busy signals are more likely, and try to avoid those times. For example, late afternoon to early evening on weekdays is often a very busy time.

- If you get disconnected from the Internet server, or if you can not access the mail server, try again right away.

- If you are waiting a lot longer than usual while the computer is trying to connect, cancel the attempt and start over.

- If you are connected, but the connection is extremely slow, disconnect and start over.

- If any problems persist—constant busy signals, frequent broken connections, and so on—contact your ISP's technical support team.

Give your ISP a chance, but if you are continually dissatisfied with their service, consider using a different ISP.

Disconnecting from the Internet

You can stay connected to the Internet as long as you want (though if you don't have unlimited service this could cost you money). Or, you can disconnect whenever you don't need to be online.

If your Internet connection ties up a phone line that you want to be available otherwise, you should disconnect when you are not using the Internet.

Here are some different ways you can disconnect:

- Right-click the connection icon at the right end of the taskbar, and select disconnect from the shortcut menu (Figure 6.5).

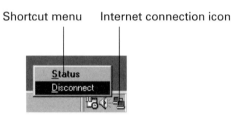

FIGURE 6.5   The Internet connection icon and shortcut menu

- When you close some Internet programs they'll ask you if you want to disconnect.
- Some connections are automatically terminated if they have been inactive for a certain amount of time. A dialog box enables you to reestablish the connection, if needed—just click the Reconnect button (Figure 6.6).

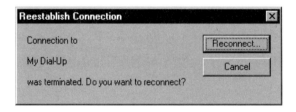

FIGURE 6.6   The Reestablish Connection dialog box

   Windows 98 offers some Internet features, such as Active Channels, for which you can schedule connections. You can set up your computer so it automatically connects to the Internet, downloads e-mail or specific Web content, and then disconnects. To learn more about e-mail features, see Chapter 7, Sending and Receiving E-Mail. To learn more about Active Channels, see Chapter 9, Using Active Web Features.

SENDING AND RECEIVING E-MAIL

7

One of the main features of the Internet is communication via e-mail. Now you can easily communicate with individuals and groups from across town to across the world. In this chapter, you'll learn how to use Outlook Express for sending and receiving e-mail, and for exploring areas of interest through newsgroups.

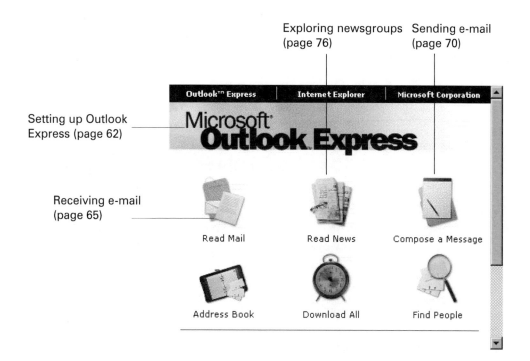

FIGURE 7.1 Communicate across town and across the world with Outlook Express

SETTING UP OUTLOOK EXPRESS

Outlook Express is the e-mail program that comes with Windows 98. Outlook Express makes it easy to communicate with the online world, using e-mail and newsgroups.

Starting Outlook Express

You can start Outlook Express using the icon in the Quick Launch toolbar in the taskbar, or the icon on the desktop.

The first time you use Outlook Express, you may get some dialog boxes asking for information.

To start Outlook Express, follow these steps:

1 Open the Outlook Express icon.

2 If you get a dialog box asking where to store messages, you can accept the default setting, which is the Outlook Express folder, or you can change it now or later. Then click OK.

3 If you get a dialog box asking if you want Outlook Express to be your default mail program, you can set it to not appear again, and then make it the default. Then click OK.

4 If you get a dialog box asking if you want to bring information in from a previous e-mail program, make the choices you want. (Unless you have a reason not to, you may as well do this.) Then click OK.

A dialog box displays asking you to select a connection.

Making the Connection

The dialog box for selecting a connection will display each time you start Outlook Express, unless you set it up to make the connection automatically. If you are using the same dial-up connection whenever you start Outlook Express, you might as well make the connection automatically (Figure 7.2).

Dial-up connection

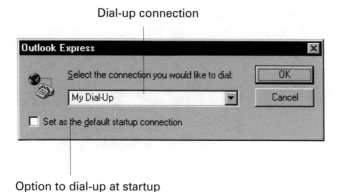

Option to dial-up at startup

FIGURE 7.2   The Outlook Express dialog box for selecting a connection

To select a connection, complete these steps:

1   Make sure your dial-up connection is selected in the dialog box.
Select from the drop-down list, if necessary.

2   If you want the connection to be dialed automatically when you start Outlook Express, check the *Set as default startup connection* option.

3   Click OK.

The computer connects to the Internet. Outlook Express is ready to send and
receive e-mail.

From now on, starting Outlook Express will automatically make the dial-up connection, and Outlook Express will automatically check for new messages.

 Once you have set Outlook Express to make the dial-up connection when
it starts, you might find some occasions when you want to start it and work
offline. To do this, you can click the Cancel button in the Connecting dialog
box while the computer is dialing.

With Outlook Express, you can:

•   **Read mail** that has been sent to you.

•   **Read news** messages that you are interested in.

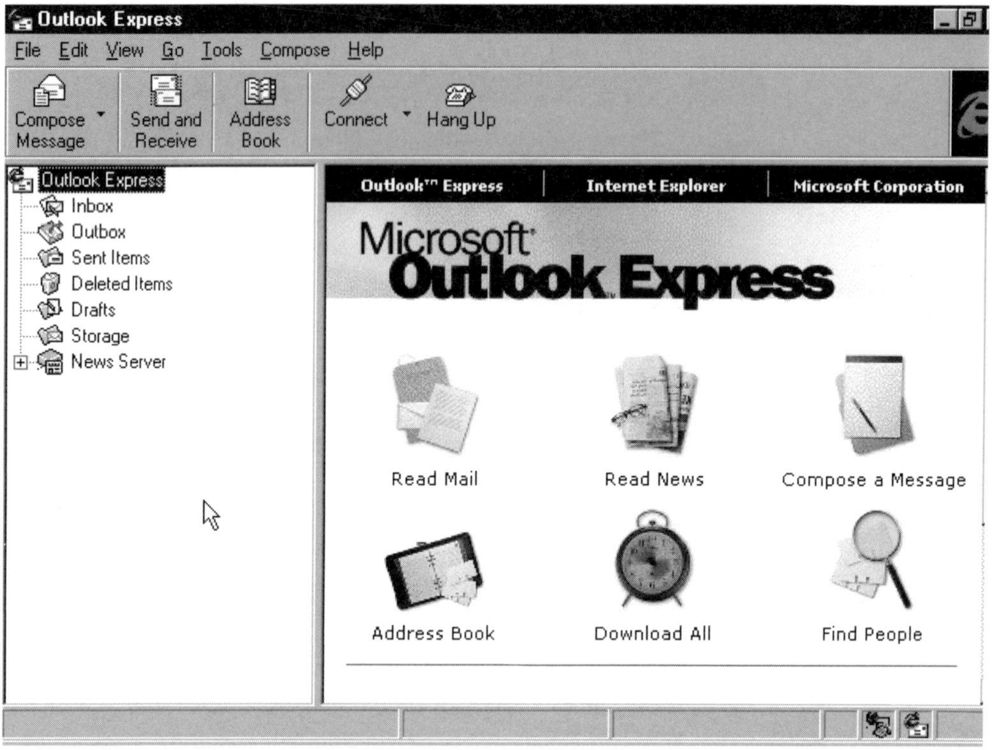

FIGURE 7.3　The Outlook Express window displays, with the main Outlook
Express screen

- **Compose a message** to send via e-mail.
- **Add or edit Address Book** entries.
- **Download all messages** that you are interested in from newsgroups.
- **Find people** on the Internet.

You can access these features from this screen, or from menus and buttons in Outlook Express (Figure 7.3). You'll learn about all of these in this chapter, except for the Find People feature, which I will cover in Chapter 8, Browsing the Web.

RECEIVING E-MAIL

When someone sends you e-mail, it is stored in an electronic mailbox on an Internet server, a computer that stores Internet information. When Outlook Express checks for e-mail, it downloads any e-mail from that server mailbox to your computer.

Downloading E-Mail Messages

To download e-mail messages from the server to your computer, follow these steps:

1 Click the Send and Receive button in the toolbar, unless e-mail is checked automatically when you start Outlook Express.

2 If the computer asks for your mail password the first time you check for e-mail, type it in, check to have the computer remember the password, and select OK.

3 If the graphic Microsoft Outlook Express startup screen displays in the right frame, click the Inbox icon in the left frame to display the Inbox.

If any e-mail is downloaded, it appears in your Inbox.

Viewing E-Mail

The message list displays in the Inbox. If the Inbox is not displayed:

Click the Inbox folder in the folder list in the left pane.

Each message in the Inbox has a header that contains key information: who sent the message, what the subject is, and when it was sent (Figure 7.4). The selected message displays in the preview pane, below the Inbox.

To view a message in the preview pane, you can:

1 Make sure the message header is selected.

2 Use the preview window scroll bars to view all of the message.

To view a message in its own window, you can:

1 Double-click the message header.

2 When you are done viewing the message, close the message window.

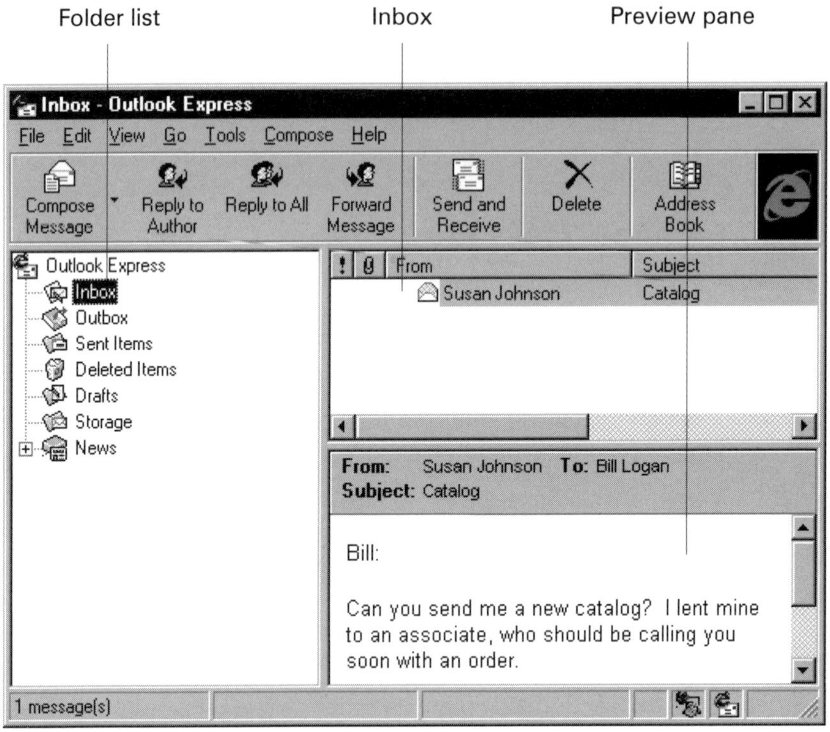

Folder list   Inbox   Preview pane

FIGURE 7.4 The Outlook Express window, with the Inbox displayed

Working with Attached Files

E-mail messages can have attached files that need to be opened in another program, for example, a word processor or spreadsheet document (Figure 7.5). A paper clip symbol in front of a message header means the message has one or more attachments.

Outlook Express provides some options for working with attached files:

- If the message is displayed in the preview window, clicking the paper clip symbol in the preview window header enables you to open and save any attached files.

- If the message is displayed in its own message window, each attachment appears as a file icon at the end of the message. Double-clicking an attachment icon enables you to open and save the attached file.

Depending on the type of file it is:

- Outlook Express may save the file in a temporary folder, and open it with the appropriate program. For example, an attached Microsoft Word document with a *.doc* extension would be opened in the Microsoft Word program, or

- Outlook Express may display a dialog box with choices for either opening the file or saving it to disk.

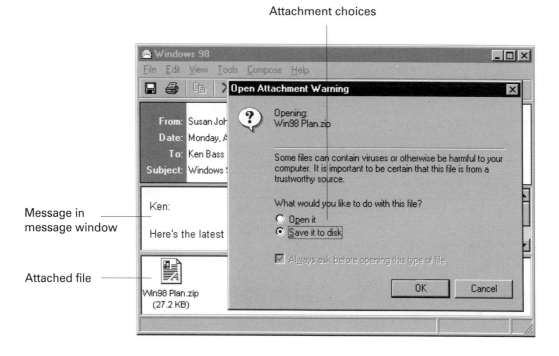

FIGURE 7.5 A message with an attachment

The dialog box includes a warning that some files can contain viruses, and that you should be sure you can trust the source of the file:

- If you choose to open the attached file, Outlook Express will look for the correct program with which to open it. If it doesn't recognize the file extension, it will ask you to select a program.

- If you choose to save the attached file, Outlook Express will ask you to select a folder in which to save it.

Managing E-Mail Messages

Often when you get a message you'll want to send out a reply to it, or forward it to someone else. Outlook Express makes that easy by offering a number of buttons for managing messages:

- **Reply to Author**—to send a reply to the selected message's author.

- **Reply to All**—to send a reply to the author and everyone else who received this e-mail.

- **Forward Message**—to send a copy of the message to another e-mail address.

You can also delete messages, or drag them to another Outlook Express folder in the left pane. It's a good idea to handle messages when they come in, storing or deleting them as appropriate, so they don't pile up in your Inbox and take up space on your hard disk.

 You can create new Outlook Express folders by opening the File menu, selecting Folder, and New Folder.

File Extensions and the Programs Associated with Them

File extensions are usually assigned by a program when you create a file. They tell Windows with what program the file should be opened. For example, the *.doc* extension is used for Microsoft Word files. Double-clicking a filename with that extension will launch Microsoft Word, and then open the file. Here is a list of common file extensions and the programs associated with them:

- AVI—Video clip
- BAT—MS-DOS batch file
- CDR—Corel Draw graphic (also CDT and PAT)
- COM—MS-DOS application
- DOC—Microsoft Word document
- DOT—Microsoft Word template
- MDB—Microsoft Access database
- MID—MIDI sound file
- PDF—Adobe Acrobat document
- PPT—Microsoft Powerpoint presentation
- QIC—Microsoft Backup backup file
- RTF—Documents saved in the Rich Text Format. These can be displayed in programs other than the one in which which they were created.
- TXT—ASCII (plain) text files that can be displayed in any program that handles text.
- WAV—Wave sound file
- WB3—Corel Quattro Pro spreadsheet (also WB1 and WB2)
- WK3—Lotus 1-2-3 spreadsheet (also WK1, WK4)
- WPD—Corel WordPerfect document
- XLS—Microsoft Excel worksheet
- ZIP—PKZIP compressed file(s)

Graphics files, while created with a particular program, can be opened in many different programs. (Not all programs can open all graphic file types.) Here is a list of some common graphics file extensions:

- BMP
- CPT
- GIF
- JPG
- PCD
- PCX
- TIF

SENDING E-MAIL

With Outlook Express, you can easily compose and send e-mail messages. You can choose stationery to send it on, get e-mail addresses from your address book, and attach files to be sent with the message.

Starting an E-Mail Message

When starting an e-mail message, you can choose whether to send it on a plain background, or on stationery. Outlook Express offers a choice of stationery, including different graphic backgrounds and fonts.

To begin composing a message, you can:

- Click the Compose button for an e-mail message on a plain background, or
- Click the Compose button arrow and choose a stationery type from the list.

The composing window opens.

The stationery displayed in Figure 7-6 has a decorative graphic border. Some e-mail programs won't be able to display stationery graphics, but they will still display the message text.

Using the Address Book

To enter an e-mail address you can type it on the To line of the New Message window, or you can use the Address Book feature.

To enter an address using the Address Book, follow these steps:

1 Click the address card icon by the To line. The Address Book opens in the Select Recipients dialog box (Figure 7.7).

2 Select the name you want from the list.

3 Click the To button to make them a recipient.

4 Click OK. The address is entered in the New Message window.

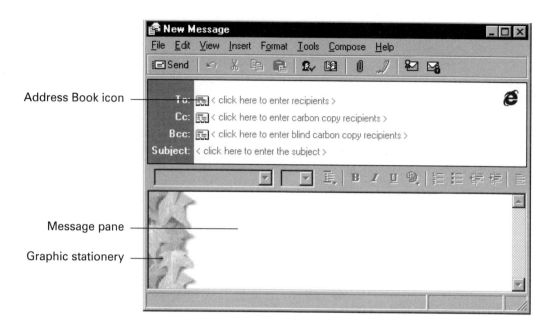

Address Book icon

Message pane

Graphic stationery

FIGURE 7.6 The New Message window, for composing e-mail

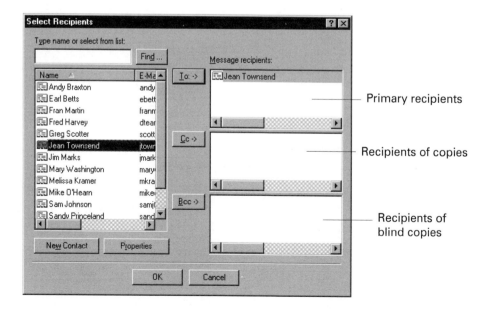

Primary recipients

Recipients of copies

Recipients of blind copies

FIGURE 7.7 The Windows 98 Address Book in the Select Recipients window

You can also select recipients for copies of the message. While all primary recipients and regular copy recipients are indicated in the message, blind copy recipients are not.

 The entries in your Address Book may have been imported from your previous e-mail program when you first started Outlook Express. You can add more with the New Contact button in the Select Recipients dialog box. You can also work directly with the Address Book by clicking the Address Book button in the Internet Explorer window.

Typing the Message

You should always include the message subject when you compose a message. The subject isn't required, but its very helpful to the recipient since it displays in the message header (Figure 7.8).

To enter the subject and message, follow these steps:

1 Click in the Subject line.

2 Type a subject.

3 Press Tab to move to the message area.

4 Type a message.

The formatting toolbar in the lower portion of the New Message window offers formatting and alignment choices for your message. Not all e-mail programs that receive a message can display this formatting, but the message text will always be displayed.

Attaching Files

You can attach document files to an e-mail message. If a document file needs to be opened in another program, such as a word processor, spreadsheet, or graphics program, you can attach it to an e-mail message.

When the recipient gets the message, they can open the attachment in the appropriate program. For information on receiving messages with attachments, see the Working with Attached Files section earlier in this chapter.

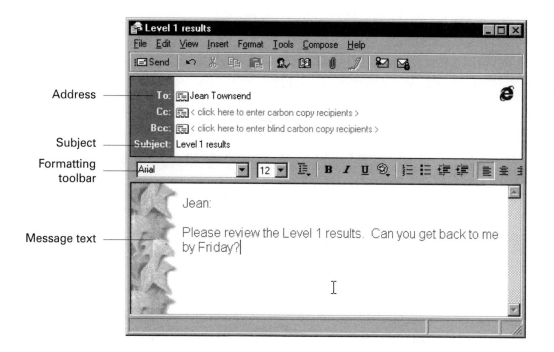

Address ——— To:
Subject ——— Subject:
Formatting toolbar ———
Message text ———

FIGURE 7.8 The New Message window with subject and message text

> **TIP**
>
> E-mail messages with large attached files can take a long time to send and receive. If you are attaching a large file, you may want to compress it first, with a program such as PKZIP. (Make sure the recipient has a program to uncompress it.) A compressed file is smaller, and will be sent and received in less time.

To attach a file to an e-mail message, follow these steps:

1 Click the Insert button in the upper toolbar of the New Message window.

2 In the Insert Attachment dialog box, browse to find the file you want to attach.

3 Double-click the file, or select it and click the Attach button.

The file is attached (Figure 7.9). An icon for the attached file displays at the bottom of the New Message window.

You can attach more than one file to an e-mail message. Simply repeat the above process for each file you want to attach.

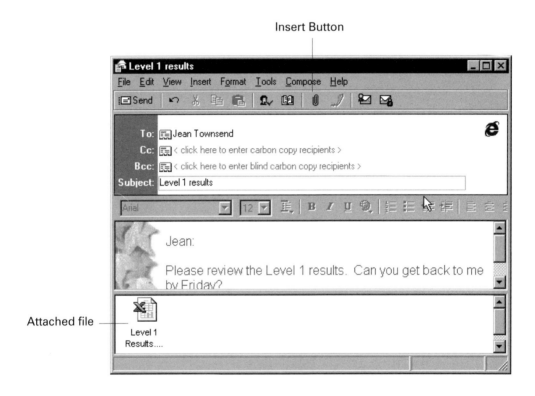

FIGURE 7.9   The New Message window with an attached file

Sending the Message

Once your message is completed, it's ready to send.

- Click the Send button.

The message is moved to the Outbox, the computer makes a connection with the mail server, and the message is sent.

Working Offline

When you are using Outlook Express, you can choose to work offline, which means that even if your computer is connected to the Internet, Outlook Express is not.

Working offline is useful if you want to read, manage, or compose e-mail without sending or receiving anything.

To work offline, just follow these steps:

1   Open the File menu in the Outlook Express window.

2   Select Work Offline (Figure 7.10).

FIGURE 7.10   The Work Offline choice on the Outlook Express File menu

When you are working offline, you have different options for sending (and receiving) messages:

- If you choose Send in the New Message window when you are working offline, the message is moved to the Outbox, and waits until the next time you send messages when you are online again.

- If you click the Send and Receive button when you are working offline, Outlook Express will ask if you want to go online. If you choose to go online, Outlook Express will send whatever is in the Outbox, and check for any new messages sent to you.

- You can work online again simply by repeating the earlier process:

    1 Open the Outlook Express File menu. The Work Offline selection is checked, showing that you are working offline.

    2 Uncheck Work Offline.

EXPLORING NEWSGROUPS

People who share a common interest form a newsgroup on the Internet. They post messages to a news server for anyone to download and read, and then respond to if they wish. Newsgroups often become extended group discussions.

When you sign up with an ISP, you generally get access to a news server in addition to the mail server. You can then read and post newsgroup messages.

Displaying a Newsgroup List

There are thousands of newsgroups on the Internet. To find the newsgroups you're interested in, you first need to see a list of available newsgroups.

To display a list of newsgroups, follow these steps:

1 Click the news server icon in the Outlook Express left pane. (You choose a name for the news server when you set up Outlook Express on your computer.)

2 If you are not subscribed to any newsgroups, a dialog box displays asking if you want to see a list of available newsgroups.

3 Click Yes.

4 If this is the first time you are accessing newsgroups, you will get a series of dialog boxes about downloading an online list of newsgroups. Answer the questions in the dialog boxes, and Outlook Express will download a list of newsgroups to your computer. (This may take a little while.)

The Newsgroups window displays (Figure 7.11). The Outlook Express toolbar now displays buttons for use with newsgroups.

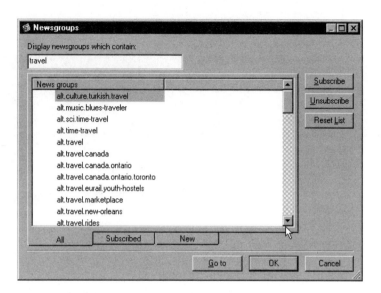

FIGURE 7.11   The Newsgroups window

Reading Newsgroup Messages

When you find a newsgroup you are interested in, you can "visit" it, that is download and read posted messages.

To visit a newsgroup, here's what you do:

1   If you want to see newsgroups on a particular subject, type a subject that could be in a newsgroup title in the Display Newsgroups Which Contain text box.

2   Select a newsgroup from the list.

3   Click the Go To button.

The headers for new messages (ones that you haven't looked at before) display in the right pane, and the newsgroup displays in the folder list in the left pane, under the news server (Figure 7.12). Newsgroups you visit display there temporarily, until you close Outlook Express. (Newsgroups you subscribe to display there permanently.)

Message headers with a plus sign next to them have replies. A sequence of replies is called a thread.

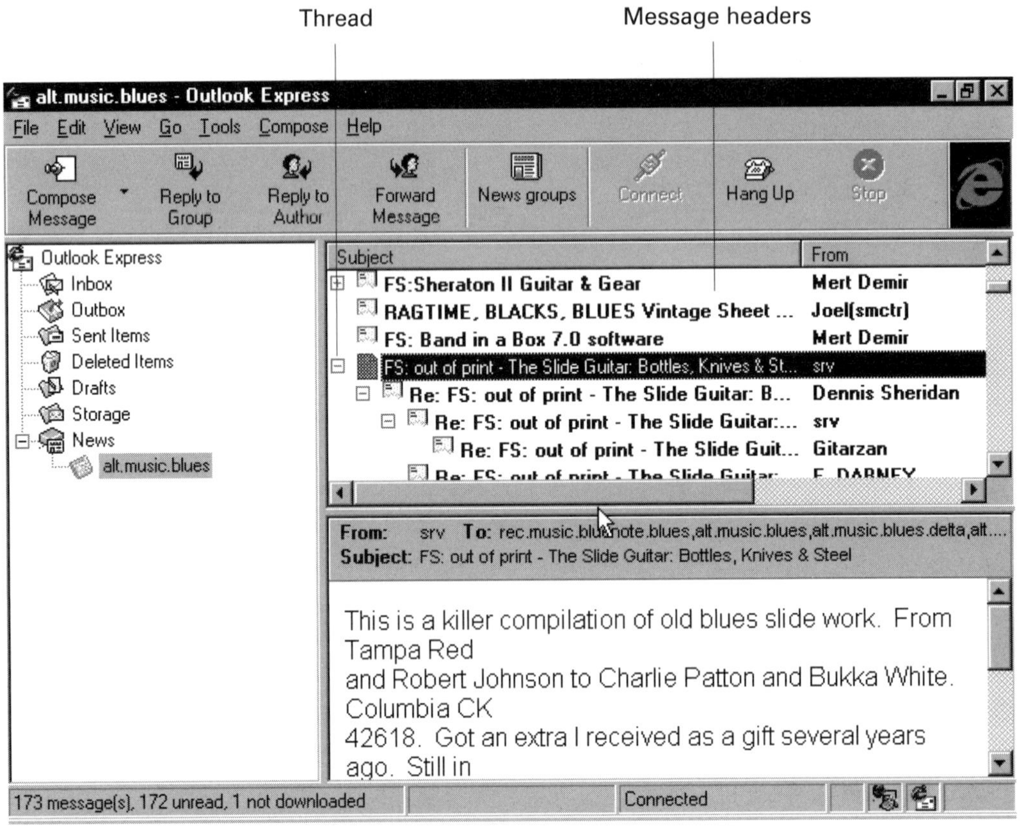

Thread   Message headers

FIGURE 7.12 Message headers, with threads

To display message threads:

> Click the plus sign next to the message.

You can follow threads, reading the messages and replies of a group conversation.

To display a message:

> Select its header.

The message content is downloaded and displays in the preview window, below the headers. (The message content is not downloaded until you select the header.)

Posting a Newsgroup Message

Once you have read some messages, and you get the feel of a newsgroup, you can post some messages yourself.

Usually you'll do that in one of two ways:

- Replying to the author of a message.
- Composing a message to post to the group.

When you reply to an author, the message becomes part of a thread, and is available to anyone who visits the site.

To reply to a message, follow these steps:

1   Select a message that you want to reply to.

2   Click the Reply to Author button in the toolbar. A window opens in which you can compose your message (Figure 7.13). The window is similar to the e-mail New Message window. The To and Subject lines are automatically filled in, and the text of the original message is included.

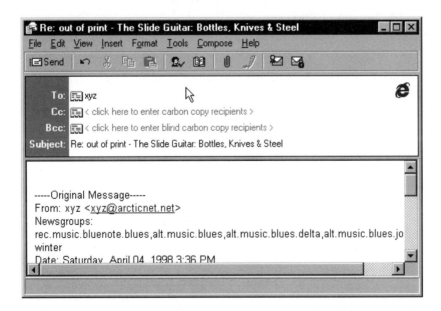

FIGURE 7.13   The message reply window

3 Type the text of your message.

4 Click the Send button.

The reply is sent.

To post a new message to the group, the process is nearly the same:

1 Click the Compose Message button. The Compose Message window opens, similar to the newsgroup reply window and the e-mail New Message window.

2 Type a subject for the message. (Newsgroup messages must have a subject.)

3 Type the text of the message.

4 Click the Post button.

The message is posted.

Subscribing to a Newsgroup

When you find a newsgroup you are interested in, you can subscribe to it, which means it's displayed in the Outlook Express folder list in the left pane, under the news server icon. Then when you want to visit it, you don't have to scroll through the list of all newsgroups in the Newgroups dialog box. Subscribing to a newsgroup doesn't cost anything.

Outlook Express offers different options for subscribing to newsgroups. If you are visiting a newsgroup you have not yet subscribed to:

1 Right-click the newsgroup in the folder list.

2 Select **Subscribe to This Newsgroup** from the shortcut menu.

If you're viewing the list of newsgroups in the Newsgroups window:

- Select the newsgroup in the list and click the Subscribe button, or
- Double-click the newsgroup in the list.

To visit a newsgroup you have subscribed to, click it in the folder list.

BROWSING THE WEB

T he World Wide Web is a fast-growing Internet feature that provides information, entertainment, products and profit to an increasing number of computer users. Windows 98 includes Internet Explorer 4.0, an integrated Web browser that provides easy access to all the features of the Web.

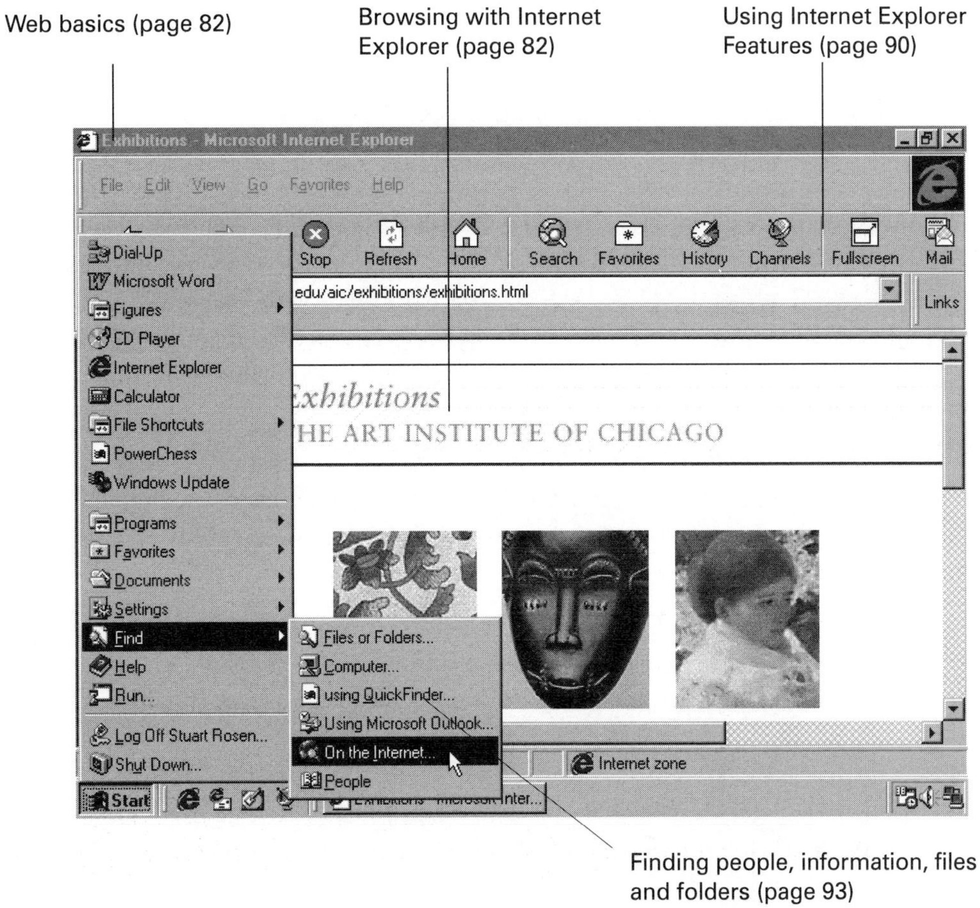

Web basics (page 82)

Browsing with Internet Explorer (page 82)

Using Internet Explorer Features (page 90)

Finding people, information, files and folders (page 93)

FIGURE 8.1   Get ready to browse the Web with Internet Explorer

WEB BASICS

The World Wide Web is an Internet service that enables you to view pages of information stored on Web servers throughout the Internet. Web pages are documents that can contain text, graphics, animation, audio, and video. When you visit a Web page, you are actually downloading a copy of that Web page to your computer.

Web pages are interconnected by hyperlinks, text or graphics that link to other Web pages. When you click a link, that page is displayed.

A set of Web pages organized together, such as the Web pages of a particular company or organization, is called a Web site. (An individual page is sometimes also referred to as a Web site.)

Web browsers are programs used to view Web pages.

BROWSING WITH INTERNET EXPLORER

Internet Explorer 4.0 is the Web browser that comes with Windows 98. You can use any Web browser with Window 98, but using Internet Explorer enables you to take full advantage of all the Web features integrated into Windows 98.

Connecting to the Internet

You can connect to the Internet and then open Internet Explorer, or you can open Internet Explorer first. Your computer may even be set up to make the dial-up connection automatically when you open Internet Explorer.

If you are logged on to a network, your Internet connection is already made.

Otherwise, make your dial-up connection by:

- Opening the dial-up icon on the desktop, if you have one.
- Selecting Start ➤ Programs ➤ Accessories ➤ Communications. Open the Dial-up Networking window and open your connection.

When you are connected, the following connection icon displays at the right end of the taskbar:

Opening Internet Explorer

The first time you start Internet Explorer, you may get some dialog boxes asking for information that Windows 98 needs to set up Internet Explorer.

To open Internet Explorer, complete these steps:

1   Open the Internet Explorer icon from the Quick Launch toolbar or from the desktop.

2   If you get a message asking if you want it to be your default browser, check the box so you won't get the message again, then click Yes.

3   If you get a dialog box asking if you want to bring information in from a previous browser, make the choices you want. (Unless you have a reason not to, you may as well do this.) Then click OK.

Internet Explorer opens, and displays your home page. Your home page is the page that Internet Explorer automatically displays when it starts.

 You can change your home page setting and other Internet Explorer settings with the Internet Options choice in the View menu.

Displaying Web Pages Using Links

A link is a reference to another Web page. Links can be text, usually underlined, or a graphic. When the mouse pointer points to a link, the pointer changes to a hand. The address (location and name) of the linked Web page displays in the Internet Explorer status bar.

To display a linked Web page:

• Click a text link

• Click a graphic link

The linked Web page displays (Figure 8.2).

 Web pages may download quickly or slowly on your computer, depending on a number of factors, including the speed of your modem and the amount of information on the page.

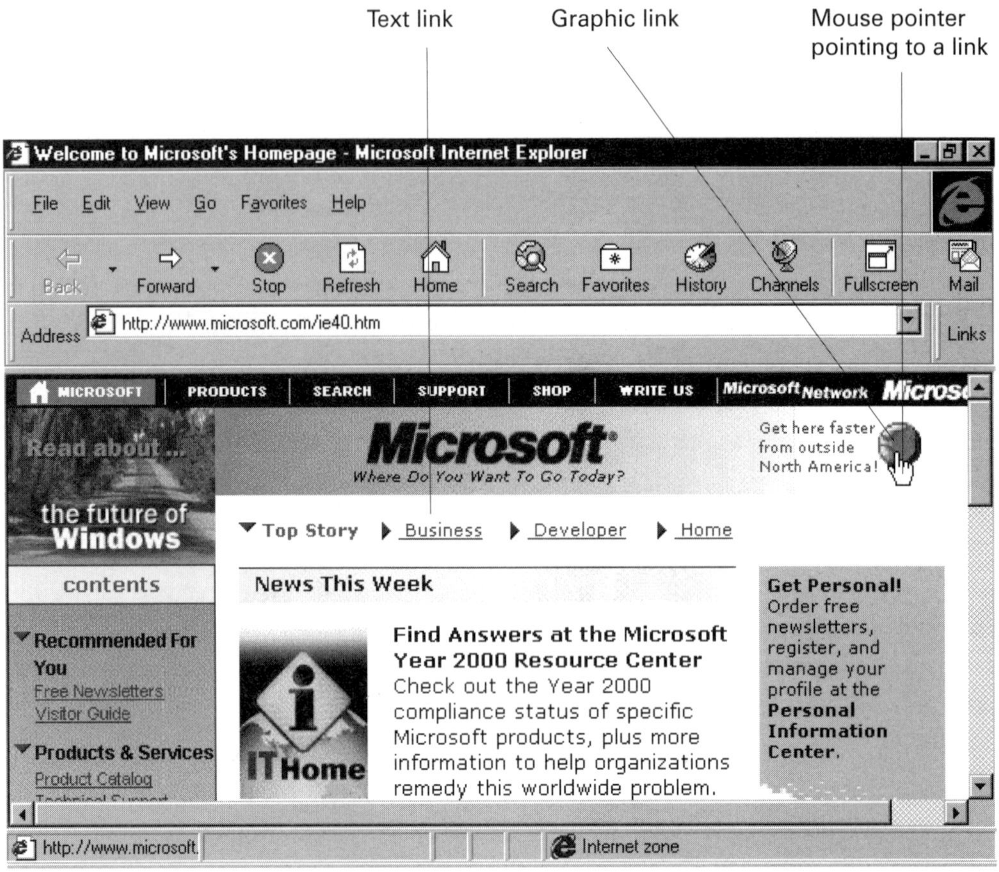

Text link   Graphic link   Mouse pointer
pointing to a link

FIGURE 8.2   The Internet Explorer window, displaying a Web page

Displaying Web Pages Using Addresses

The Address box displays the address of the current Web page. The technical term for the address is URL, for Universal Resource Locator. It includes the name of the page, preceded by its location on the Internet.

When you get information about a Web site—from a friend, an ad, and so on—make sure you get its URL. Then you can view that page by using the address information.

Web addresses start with *http://*, and usually, but not always, continue with *www*. When entering addresses in Internet Explorer you can skip the *http://*, and start typing with whatever follows.

For example, for the U.S. House of Representatives Web page, the address is:

www.house.gov/

The Internet Explorer Address box ———

To display a page using its address, follow these steps:

1   Type a Web address in the Address box.

 The AutoComplete feature matches up what you are typing with addresses you have already visited. If it finds a match, it completes the address for you.

2   When the address is typed in, press Enter.

The Web page displays.

Revisiting Pages with the Back and Forward Buttons

The Back and Forward buttons in the toolbar move through the Web pages you have looked at. Both buttons have dropdown lists of visited pages (Figure 8.3).

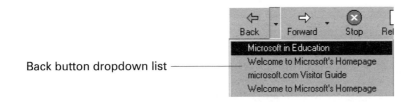

Back button dropdown list

F I G U R E 8.3   Back and Forward buttons, with a dropdown list

To move back through Web pages you have visited:

- Click the Back button.
- To go directly to a Web page you have visited:

    1 Click the Back button dropdown arrow.

    2 Select a Web page from the list.

To move forward through Web pages you have visited (after you have moved back):

- Click the Forward button.

(If you don't have any pages to revisit, browse through different Web pages before using these features, so you have some Web history.)

 You don't need to be online to view recently visited Web pages. When you download a page, Internet Explorer stores a copy of that page for a set number of days in a storage cache. When you use the Back and Forward buttons, or the History feature, those stored pages are displayed from the cache.

Revisiting Pages with the History Bar

The History bar displays links to pages you have recently visited, organized by day.

To revisit a Web page with the History bar, just complete these steps:

1 Click the History button in the toolbar. The History bar displays in the left pane, with a list of recently visited Web pages organized by day and by Web site (Figure 8.4).

2 In the History bar, click a day and site to xdisplay a Web page address.

3 Click the address.

The page displays in the right pane.

 To remove the History bar, or any other Explorer bar, from the left pane, just click its button again.

Visiting Favorite Web Pages

The Favorites feature in Windows 98 enables you to keep a list of favorite Web pages (and favorite files and folders on your computer). You can select a favorite from the

FIGURE 8.4 The Internet Explorer History bar

list, and display it. This gives you a quick way to view Web pages (and files and folders) that you use often.

To visit a favorite Web page, just follow these steps:

1 Click the Favorites button in the toolbar. The Favorites bar displays in the left pane, with favorite items organized in folders (Figure 8.5).

 You may have an Imported Bookmarks folder in your favorites bar. If so, it was created when you first used Internet Explorer, by importing bookmarks from a browser you were using previously.

2 Display a Web page name in the left pane.

3 Click the address.

The page displays in the right pane.

 You can also display your favorites list from the Favorites menu in the menu bar or from the Start menu.

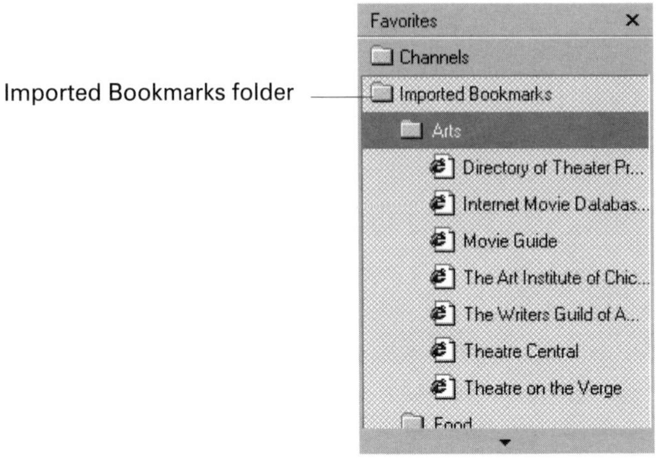

Imported Bookmarks folder ———

FIGURE 8.5 The Internet Explorer Favorites bar

Adding Favorites

It's easy to add Web page locations, as well as files and folders, to your favorites list.

To add a Web page to the favorites list, follow these steps:

1   Make sure the Web page you want to add is displayed in the browser.

2   Open the Favorites menu in the menu bar.

3   Select Add to Favorites. The Add Favorite dialog box appears, asking if you would like to subscribe to the page (Figure 8.6). When you subscribe, you can set up automatic update information and downloading. (To learn more about subscribing to a Web page, see Chapter 9, Using Active Web Features.)

4   If you just want to add the page to your favorites, make sure that option is checked.

5   Click OK.

The Web page is added to your favorites.

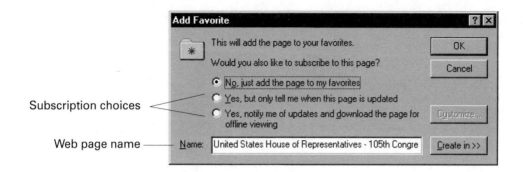

Subscription choices

Web page name

FIGURE 8.6   The Add Favorite dialog box

   You can organize the favorites in your list with the Organize Favorites choice on the Favorites menu.

Searching for Web Pages

Sometimes you want to find a particular Web page, or you want to find Web pages on a subject you are interested in, but you don't have a Web address. In those situations, you can search for Web pages for which you don't have addresses. The Internet offers a number of search services, often called search engines, that can help you find what you want.

To search for a Web page, follow these steps:

1   Click the Search button in the toolbar. The Search bar displays in the left pane (Figure 8.7). You can choose from a number of different search services in the Select Provider list.

2   In the text box, type in a word or phrase that relates to what you want to find.

3   Press Enter, or click the button that starts the search.

4   You may get a dialog box cautioning you about others being able to see information you are sending. Unless this is a serious concern for you, select Yes to continue.

Select Provider list

Search text box

FIGURE 8.7 The Internet Explorer Search bar

The browser displays a list of Web pages whose names, descriptions, or sometimes even contents contain what you are looking for. Select pages from this list to view, to find what you are looking for.

 Most search Web pages also provide lists of topics or categories that you can browse through, to focus your search.

USING INTERNET EXPLORER FEATURES

Internet Explorer comes with a series of features that help you make the most of your browsing experience.

Working with Toolbars

The Internet Explorer standard toolbar includes buttons to control the way Internet Explorer looks and works (Figure 8.8).

FIGURE 8.8   Internet Explorer toolbar buttons

Here is a description of the buttons that have not yet been covered in this chapter:

Stop—Stops the downloading process.

Refresh—Reloads the current page. Use the Refresh feature to display the most current version of a Web page.

Home—Returns you to your home page.

Fullscreen—Maximizes the size of the Web page. To use the Fullscreen feature, click the Fullscreen button. The Web page fills the screen, so that only the standard toolbar remains (without text labels). If you want to display the Taskbar, point to the bottom of the screen. To return the screen to its normal view, click the Fullscreen button again.

Mail—Opens your e-mail program.

NOTE You can set which program the Mail button opens (for example, Outlook Express) by selecting Internet Options from the View menu, and going to the Programs tab.

TIP If you don't have a Mail button, close Internet Explorer and then reopen it, after you have set your mail program.

Print—Prints the current page.

Edit—Opens FrontPad, a program you can use to create and edit Web pages.

NOTE Internet Explorer provides a Links toolbar that includes links to some useful Web sites. The Links toolbar on your computer may be positioned at the right of the Address bar, and mostly hidden. You can move and resize toolbars by dragging the vertical bar at the left end of the toolbar. For example, you could move the Links toolbar under the Address bar by dragging it there.

Browsing Files On Your Hard Disk

The Internet Explorer window looks and works a lot like the Windows Explorer window. You can display folder contents in the Internet Explorer window the same way you display a Web page. In fact, Internet Explorer is basically the same feature as Windows Explorer.

To display a folder in Internet Explorer, you can:

- Select a folder from the Favorites list, or
- Type and enter a folder location and name in the Address box, or
- Select a disk drive from the Address box dropdown list, and then select a folder.

When a folder displays in Internet Explorer, the "smart" toolbar changes to the Windows Explorer toolbar.

You can display a Web page again with standard Internet Explorer methods: Address box, Back and Forward buttons, and so on. You can display the Explorer bars from the View menu. When you go back to a Web page, the smart toolbar changes accordingly.

Screening Internet Content

Since the Web contains such a variety of information, you may feel that some content is inappropriate for children. Internet Explorer's Content Advisor helps you control the types of content that your computer can access on the Internet. When the Content Advisor is enabled, only content that meets or exceeds your standards can be accessed.

To enable the Content Advisor, follow these steps:

1 From the View menu, choose Internet Options.

2 In the dialog box, select the Content tab.

3 In the Content Advisor box, select Enable and follow the instructions.

Content Advisor settings are password protected, so they can't be changed without your approval.

FINDING PEOPLE, INFORMATION, FILES, AND FOLDERS

Since your computer holds thousands of files, it's easy to misplace a file, or forget a file name. Now that Windows 98 has made working with the Internet easier than ever, you will be keeping track of even more information.

The Windows 98 Find utility helps you find people and information on the Web, as well as files and folders on your computer (or on a netork).

Finding People on the Internet

Windows 98 helps you find people on the Internet by linking you to several directories, including your own e-mail address book.

To use the Find utility to find people on the Internet, follow these steps:

1 From the Windows 98 Start menu, select Find.

2 From the Find menu, select People. The Find People dialog box opens.

3 From the Look In pull-down list, select an Internet directory or your own e-mail address book (Figure 8.9).

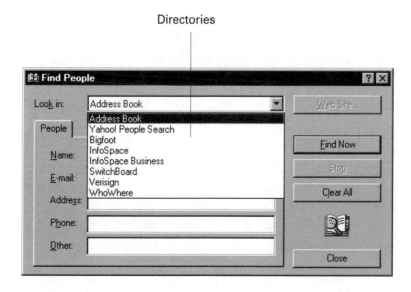

FIGURE 8.9 The Find People dialog box helps you search for people

4 Type the information you know about the person.

5 Press Enter, or click Find Now.

If the service finds any matches, they are displayed at the bottom of the dialog box.

 To view the Internet directory's Web site, click the Web Site button in the dialog box.

Finding Information on the Internet

Windows 98 helps you find information on the Internet by linking you to search services, Internet White Pages, and Yellow Pages, and other resources.

To use the Find utility to find information on the Internet, follow these steps:

1 Select Start ➤ Find ➤ On the Internet. Windows automatically launches your Web browser and connects to the Internet, if necessary, and then displays a Web page with search engine features at the top of the window.

2 Scroll the bottom of the window to see additional search sites including White Pages, Yellow Pages, and newsgroups (Figure 8.10).

3 Select the site you want to use. A form for entering information displays at the top of the window.

4 Fill in information in the form that will help find what you are looking for.

5 Start the search.

The search site will find any matches it can, and display them in the browser.

Finding a File or Folder

You can also use the Find utility to find files or folders on your computer, or your network. You can search on the name of a file or folder, a part of the name, or the last modification date. The Find utility also includes full-text search capability, in case you don't remember a file name, but know a distinctive word or phrase contained in it.

To find a file or folder by its name, follow these steps:

1 Select Start ➤ Find ➤ Files or Folders.

Search sites   Search form

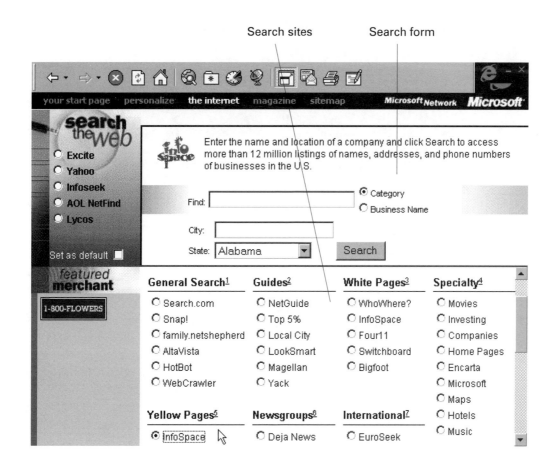

F I G U R E 8.10   The Find utility helps you search for information on the Internet

2   In the Find: All Files window, type as much as you can remember of the file or folder name in the Named box (Figure 8.11).

3   Press Enter or click Find Now.

Any files or folders that match or include what you typed are displayed at the bottom of the window. You can open those files or folders from this window.

 To limit the scope of a search to a particular folder or subfolder, click the Browse button and select the appropriate location.

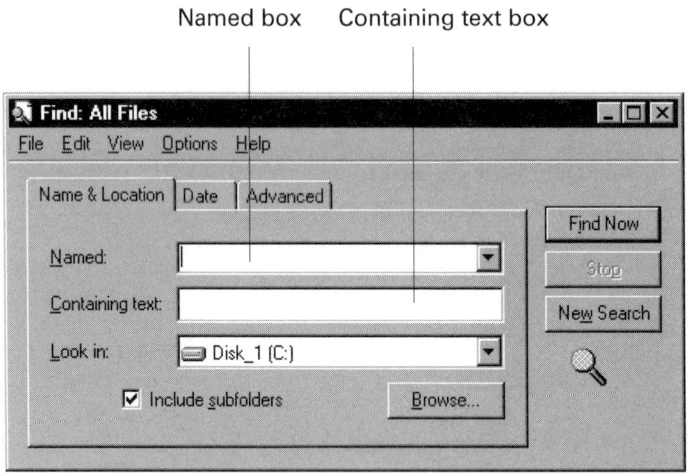

Named box   Containing text box

FIGURE 8.11   The Find: All Files window helps you search for files and folders.

To find a file by text it contains, follow these steps:

1   Make sure the Find: All Files window is open.

2   In the Containing Text box, type a distinctive word or phrase that would be contained in the file.

> **NOTE**   Type a phrase in quotes, for example, "New England," or the search will look for the words separately.

3   Press Enter or click Find Now.

Any files that contain what you typed are displayed at the bottom of the window. You can open those files from this window.

> **TIP**   For a case-sensitive search, open the Options menu and select Case Sensitive. Repeat the process to deselect the option.

> **NOTE**   When you open a file or folder from the list in the Find: All Files window, the window automatically closes. To keep it open so you can look at other files or folders from the list, make sure Save Results is checked in the Options menu.

9

USING ACTIVE WEB FEATURES

· ·

S̲ome of the most exciting features of Windows 98 are the active Web features. You can schedule automatic deliveries of Web content with Active Channels, and you can display up-to-the-minute Web content on the Active Desktop.

Adding Web elements to the Active Desktop (page 103)

Subscribing to Active Channels (page 98)

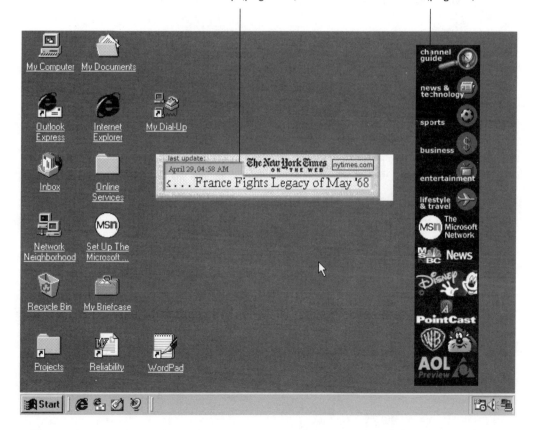

FIGURE 9.1   Take advantage of Windows 98 active Web features

SUBSCRIBING TO ACTIVE CHANNELS

A channel is a Web site specially designed to deliver content to your computer. You can subscribe to a channel, which sets up a schedule for how and when the content is automatically delivered to your computer. Subscribing to a channel doesn't cost anything extra, it just means scheduled delivery.

Active channels provide an ideal way to have updated Web information downloaded to your computer when you want—during the night, for example, when the Internet system is less busy. Then you can look at it whenever it is convenient for you, without having to be online.

Displaying the Channel Bar on the Desktop

The Channel bar displays on the desktop to give you easy access to channels. If the Channel bar is not displayed on your desktop, make sure the desktop is set to display as a Web page.

To display the desktop as a Web page, follow these steps:

1 Right-click an empty area of the desktop.

2 From the shortcut menu, select **Active Desktop**.

3 Make sure **View As Web Page** is checked in the submenu.

If the Channel bar still does not display, it needs to be turned on in your display settings. To turn on the Channel bar, follow these steps:

1 Right-click an empty area of the desktop.

2 From the shortcut menu, select **Active Desktop**.

3 From the submenu, select **Customize My Desktop**. The Display Properties dialog box opens, with the Web tab selected. The upper part shows the layout of active Web elements on the desktop. The lower part shows what active Web elements have been set up.

4 Select Internet Explorer Channel Bar. (Figure 9.2)

5 Click OK.

The Channel bar displays on the desktop.

The Channel bar shows the channels installed on your computer. That doesn't mean you have subscribed to them, it just means they are available to you. The

Active Desktop elements   Layout of active Web elements

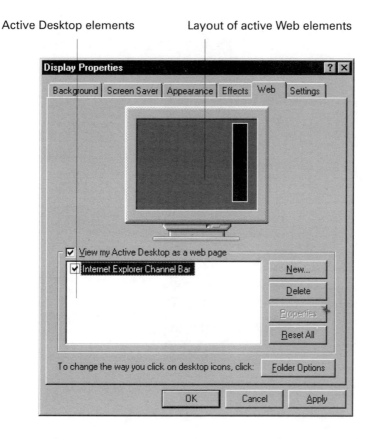

FIGURE 9.2   The Display Properties dialog box, with the Web tab selected

Channel bar features individual channels at the bottom, channel categories above them, and the Channel Guide at the top.

Subscribing to an Active Channel

You can look at the channels on your Channel bar, and subscribe to any you are interested in. To view a channel, you can select it in the Channel bar, or you can start by selecting a category in the Channel bar (Figure 9.3).

To view a channel from a category, just follow these steps:

1   Make sure you are connected to the Internet (or that Internet Explorer connects automatically when it opens).

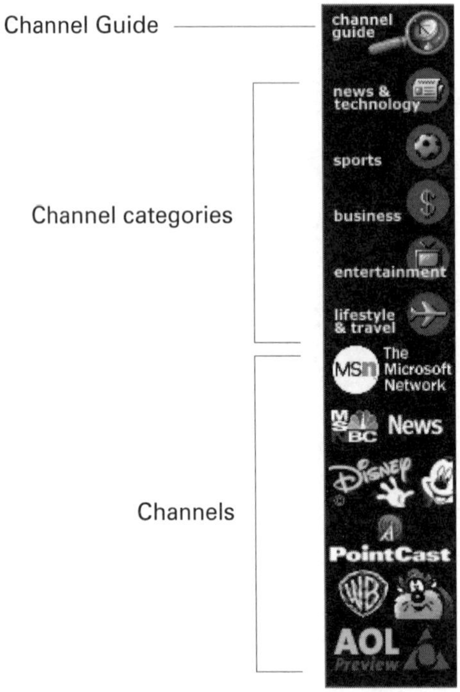

Channel Guide ————————

Channel categories

Channels

FIGURE 9.3   The Channel bar on the desktop

2   Click a category in the Channel bar. The Internet Explorer window displays in fullscreen mode (Figure 9.4). The Channel bar displays to the left. Icons for the channels in the category you selected display in the Channel bar, and in the browser window.

NOTE The Channel bar (and any other Explorer bar) will slide off the screen to the left when Internet Explorer is in fullscreen mode. Whenever you want to display it, just point to the left side of the window.

3   Click a channel you're interested in (in the Channel bar or the browser window). The introductory page for that channel displays. The page shows options to add it to the Active Desktop, or to add it as an Active Channel (Figure 9.5). Some pages also offer more than one content choice. (For more about the Active Desktop, see Adding Web Elements to the Active Desktop, later in this chapter.)

Channel bar   Channels

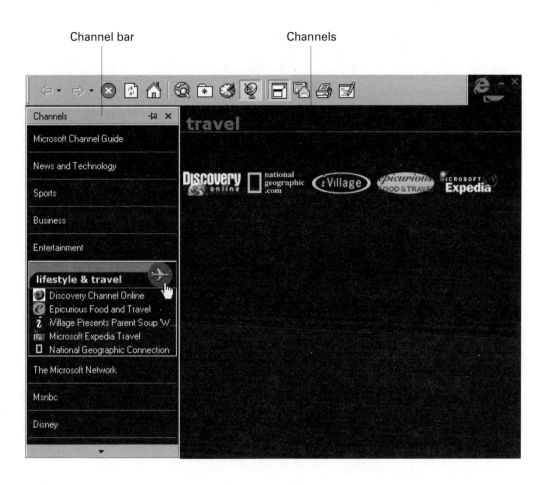

FIGURE 9.4   The Internet Explorer window, with the Channel bar and channel icons

4   Click the Add Active Channel option for the content you want. A dialog
box asks about subscribing, and offers three choices (Figure 9.6):

- Don't subscribe, but add it to the Channel bar
- Subscribe so that you are notified when the channel information
  gets updated
- Subscribe, get notified of updates, and have the information
  downloaded

Add Active Channel button   Channel introductory page

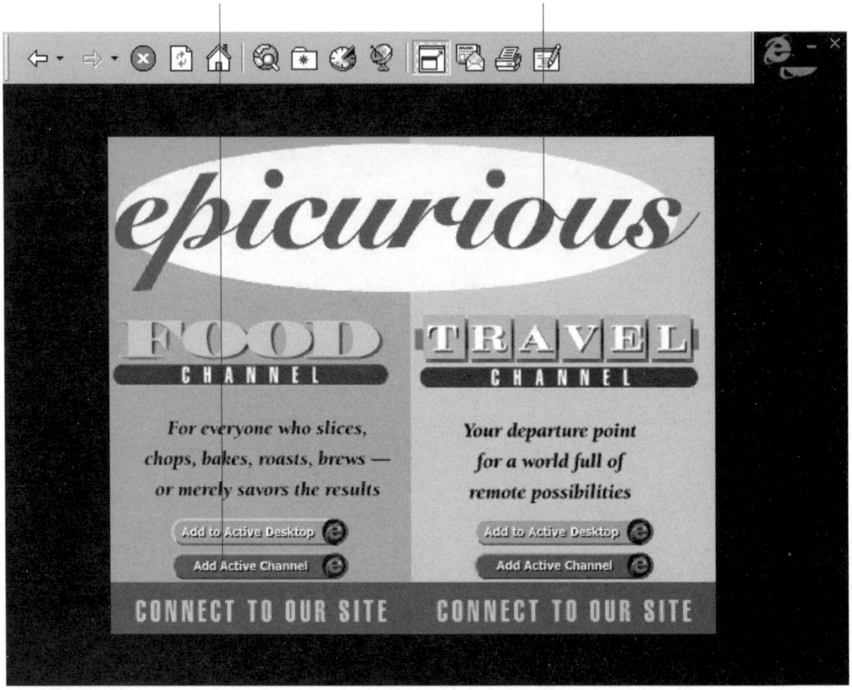

FIGURE 9.5   A channel introductory page, with active Web options

 Choosing the download option means that channel content will be auto-matically downloaded to your computer according to the publisher's recommended update schedule (usually during the late night or early morning). You can view and change that and other settings with the Customize button.

5   To accept the default settings, click OK.

6   In the Channel Screen Saver dialog box, select whether or not you want a channel content screen saver to replace your current screen saver.

The channel subscription is complete. At the scheduled time, your computer will automatically connect to the Internet, visit the channel site, download new content, and disconnect from the Internet (as long as your computer is running).

Subscription choices

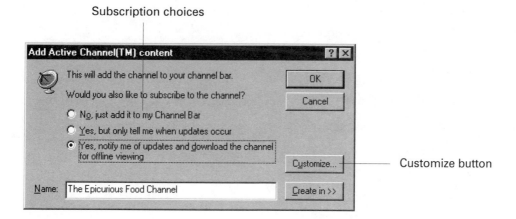

Customize button

FIGURE 9.6   The Add Active Channel content dialog box

 New channels are regularly being offered by content providers, and you can keep up with the latest channels by using the Channel Guide. Selecting the Channel Guide button in the Channel bar, or the View Channels button in the taskbar, takes you to Microsoft's Channel Guide Web site. There you can see any new channels, and add the ones you want to your Channel bar. Some content providers offer access to channels directly from their Web sites.

ADDING WEB ELEMENTS TO THE ACTIVE DESKTOP

With the Windows 98 Active Desktop, you can turn Web elements into desktop elements. With the Active Desktop you can stay current with your favorite Web-based content, such as news, weather, traffic reports or financial information. It has never been more convenient to bring elements from the Internet to your desktop and into your workday.

Adding Channel Content to the Active Desktop

Many Active Channel providers offer options for adding channel content to the Active Desktop.

First, your desktop needs to be set to display as a Web page. If you are not sure, just follow these steps:

1   Right-click an empty area of the desktop.

2   From the shortcut menu, select **Active Desktop**.

3   Make sure **View As Web Page** is checked in the submenu.

To choose a channel to add to the desktop, follow these steps:

1   Select a channel from the Channel bar, or from a Channel bar category.

2   From the channel introductory page, select **Add to Active Desktop** for the content you want.

3   If you get a security message making sure you want to add this to the desktop, click Yes. A dialog box gives the name and URL of the channel, and makes sure you want to subscribe.

4   Click OK.

5   Click the Show Desktop button in the taskbar.

The active Web element displays on the Active Desktop.

Some Active Desktop elements update automatically while you are online. To update Web elements whenever you want to, follow these steps:

1   Display the desktop shortcut menu (Figure 9.7)

2   Select **Active Desktop**.

3   Select **Update Now**. The content is updated.

> **TIP**   With many Active Desktop elements, you can click information they display to open a Web page with related information.

> **NOTE**   You can add Web page content to your Active Desktop by right-clicking and dragging a link or a graphic from the browser window to the desktop.

Changing the Active Desktop

Once you have Web elements on the Active Desktop, you have a number of options for changing the desktop.

To move an element around on the desktop, drag the bar at the top.

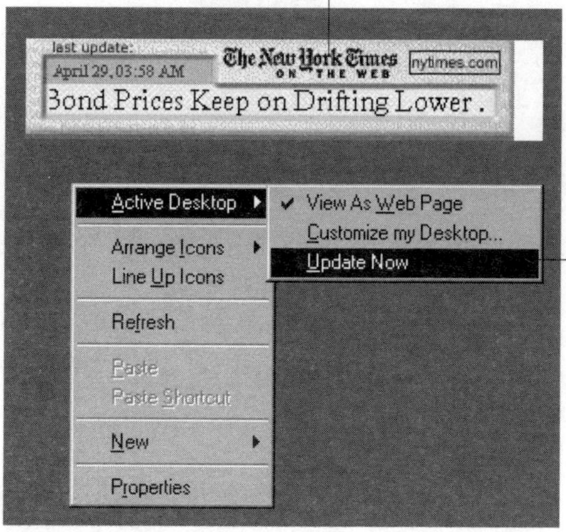

Active Web element

Update Now option

FIGURE 9.7 An Active Desktop element and the desktop shortcut menu

To turn particular Web elements on or off, follow these steps:

1 Point to a Web element. A bar displays at the top of the element.

2 Click the X button in the bar. The element is turned off.

To control Web elements from the Display Properties dialog box, follow these steps:

1 Right-click an empty area of the desktop.

2 From the shortcut menu display the **Active Desktop** submenu.

3 Select **Customize My Desktop.**

4 In the Display Properties dialog box, make sure the Web tab is selected (Figure 9.8).

The options in this screen include:

- To turn an element on, make sure the element is checked.

- To remove it permanently, select it and click the Delete button.

- To add an element from a Web page or the Active Desktop Gallery, click the New button.

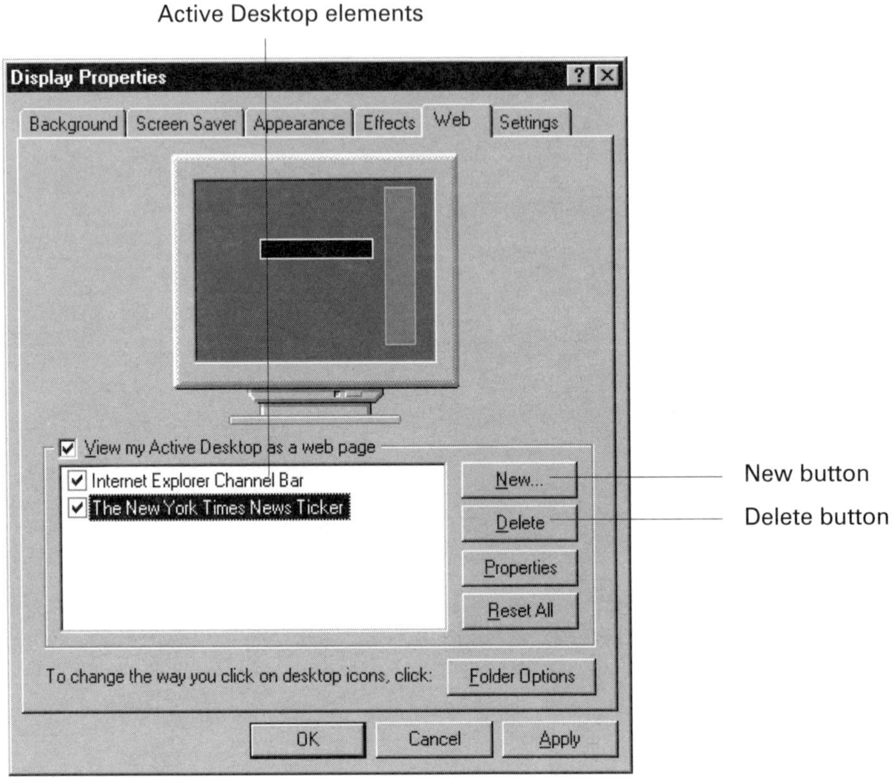

Active Desktop elements

FIGURE 9.8   The Display Properties dialog box with the Web tab selected

To set the desktop so desktop icons don't display when the Active Desktop is turned on, follow these steps:

1   Display the Effects tab in the Display Properties dialog box.

2   Select the option to hide desktop icons when the desktop is viewed as a Web page.

To switch between the active and standard desktops, simply check or uncheck the View As Web Page selection from the Active Desktop submenu in the desktop shortcut menu.

PERSONALIZING WINDOWS 98

. . . .

10

Windows 98 can be personalized to suit your style, and the way you work. It has a wide range of features you can personalize. In this chapter I will change some appearance features of Windows, including desktop colors and background. I will also change some Windows functionality, including adding shortcuts and customizing the taskbar.

Personalizing Windows functionality (page 113)

Personalizing Windows appearance (page 108)

FIGURE 10.1   Personalize Windows 98 to suit your style and the way you work

PERSONALIZING WINDOWS 98 APPEARANCE

You do a lot of work on the Windows 98 desktop, and it should be a space you can be comfortable in. You can personalize the appearance of Windows 98 as you would personalize your office.

Changing Colors

Everyone has different color preferences. In Windows 98 you can select the color scheme that you want to work in (Figure 10.2).

To change colors, follow these steps:

1 Right-click the desktop.

2 Select **Properties** from the shortcut menu.

3 In the Display Properties dialog box, click the Appearance tab.

In the Appearance screen you can select a desktop element from the preview window in the top half of the screen, then change its color, size, and font with the settings in the bottom half.

You can change the entire color scheme with these steps:

1 Open the Scheme dropdown list.

2 Select a color scheme. The scheme is previewed at the top of the window.

3 When you find a color scheme you like, click OK. The color scheme is applied to your desktop.

You can change color schemes whenever you want, and you can create your own color schemes by changing the settings of individual desktop elements, and then saving the scheme with the Save As button, giving it a name of your choice.

 If you want to preview your selection on your desktop, click the Apply button. Your selection displays temporarily. If you click Cancel, the desktop will not be changed.

Desktop preview   Save As button

Color scheme list   Desktop element settings

FIGURE 10.2   The Appearance tab in the Display Properties dialog box

Changing the Desktop Background

You can change your desktop background by adding a (repeated) pattern, such as bricks or plaid, or adding a different background or wallpaper. Patterns use the color currently selected for the desktop background.

To add a different background to your desktop, follow these steps:

1 Right-click the desktop, and select **Properties** from the shortcut menu.

2 In the Display Properties dialog box, make sure the Background tab is selected (Figure 10.3).

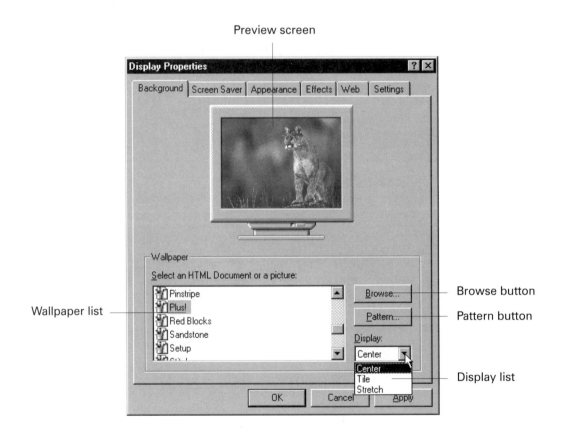

FIGURE 10.3 The Background tab in the Display Properties dialog box

3   Select a wallpaper from the Wallpaper list. The wallpaper is displayed in the preview screen.

4   If the wallpaper element is small, open the Display list and select Tile. Copies of the image will be tiled to fill the screen.

5   Click OK. The wallpaper covers your desktop background.

If you want to use a pattern for your desktop background, follow these steps:

1   In the Display Properties Background tab, make sure None is selected in the Wallpaper list. (Wallpaper covers any pattern.)

2   Click the Pattern button.

3   Select a pattern from the pattern list.

4   Click OK in the pattern list box, and in the Background tab. The pattern is applied to the desktop.

NOTE   You can create your own wallpaper by using a favorite graphic file. On the standard desktop you can use bitmap files (*.bmp),* and on the Active Desktop you can use many graphic file types, including bitmap (*.bmp*), GIF (*.gif*), and JPEG (*.jpg*) images. You can even use a Web page as wallpaper on the Active Desktop. Just use the Browse button on the Background tab to find the file you want to use.

TIP   You can turn a Web page graphic into wallpaper by right-clicking on the graphic in the browser window, and selecting the wallpaper choice from the shortcut menu.

Choosing a Screen Saver

While screen savers are not a necessity with current monitors, they give you a bit of privacy at the office and they are a fun way to personalize your computer. Windows 98 comes with several screen saver options, and almost limitless possibilities for customizing them.

To set up a screen saver, complete these steps:

1   Right-click the desktop, and select **Properties** from the shortcut menu.

2   In the Display Properties dialog box, select the Screen Saver tab (Figure 10.4).

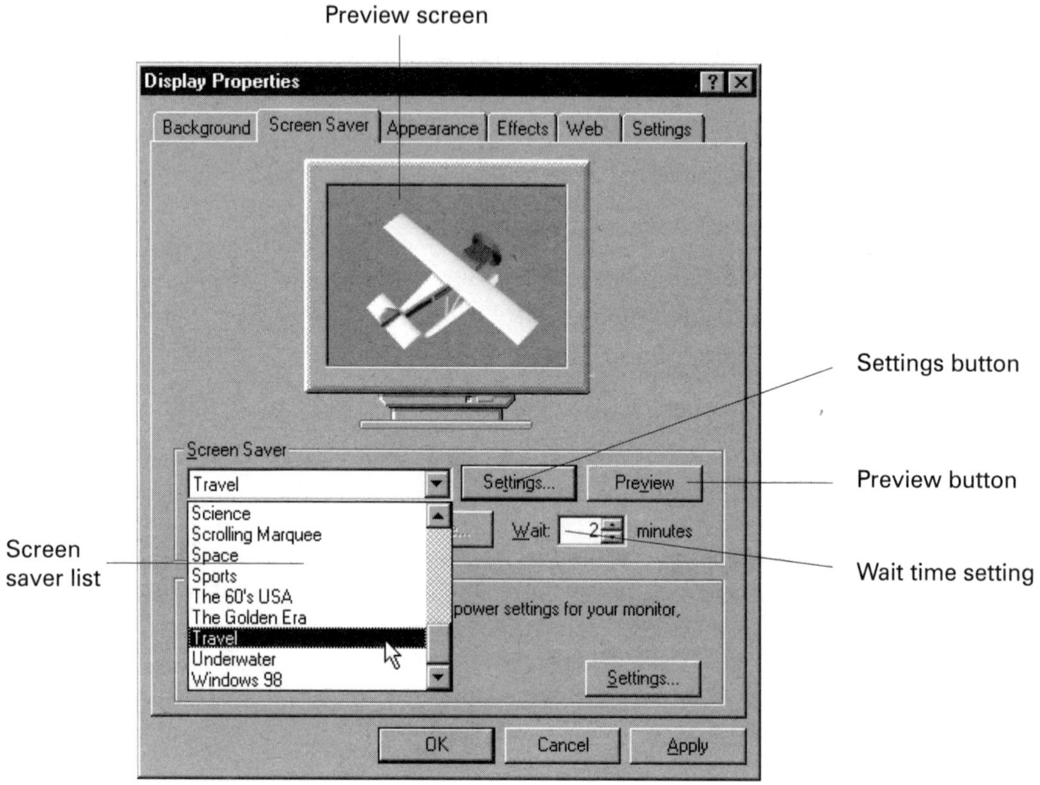

Preview screen

FIGURE 10.4   The Screen Saver tab in the Display Properties dialog box

3   Select a screen saver from the list. It previews in the dialog box preview screen.

4   If you want to customize your screen saver settings, click Settings and choose from the options in the dialog box.

5   If you want to reset the wait time before the screen saver starts, change the number in the Wait box.

6   If you want to preview the full screen saver, click the Preview button.

7   Click OK to accept your settings.

After the computer is inactive for the set amount of time, the screen saver will start. Moving your mouse or pressing any key will clear the screen saver.

 You can personalize your desktop with a themed package of appearance (and sound) elements, with the Desktop Themes feature. You'll find it in the Control Panel (Start ➤ Settings ➤ Control Panel).

PERSONALIZING WINDOWS 98 FUNCTIONALITY

As you work with Windows 98, you'll sometimes find that you wish you could change it, so it worked more the way you want it to work. You can customize the functionality in Windows 98, to make Windows 98 work more the way you do.

Creating Shortcuts

One of the most common ways in which people want to personalize Windows 98 is to have icons on the desktop for the programs, folders, and documents they use often. Windows 98 makes it easy to create shortcuts that give you quick access to the items you use.

To create a desktop shortcut, follow these steps:

1 Select Start ➤ Programs ➤ Windows Explorer.

2 Browse to find an item for which you want to create a shortcut. (It can be a program, a folder, or a document.)

3 Right-click the item.

4 In the shortcut menu, point to **Send To** (Figure 10.5).

5 From the submenu, select **Desktop as Shortcut**.

6 Display your desktop.

A shortcut icon for the item is displayed on the desktop.

 You can use the same method to create a desktop shortcut for an item in the Start menu or its submenus.

F I G U R E 10.5   Creating a desktop shortcut

You can create a shortcut in a folder that accesses an item in another location. To create a shortcut this way, follow these steps:

1   Right-click an item in a folder.

2   In the shortcut menu, select **Create Shortcut**. A shortcut is created in the folder.

Now you can move and rename the icon as you would any file or folder icon.

Adding Items to the Start Menu

You can easily add items to your Start menu and its submenus. Some people find it more convenient to have the items they use often on their Start menu, rather than their desktop.

To add an item to the Start menu, just follow these steps:

1   Make sure the item is displayed in a folder or on the desktop.

2   Drag the item to the Start button, but don't release the mouse button. The Start menu opens.

3 Drag the item to a location on the Start menu, or to any of the submenus (except Documents, Settings, or Find).

4 Release the mouse button. The item is added to the menu.

 You can reposition an item on the Start menu, or its submenus, by dragging the item, and you can delete an item by using the right-click shortcut menu.

Resizing the Taskbar

With Windows 98, you can have many programs and folders open at the same time. This can be very useful, but sometimes your taskbar can become full of buttons that are small and hard to read. To resize the taskbar, complete these steps:

1 Point to the top edge of the taskbar. The pointer displays as a double-headed arrow.

2 Drag the point up slightly. The taskbar expands to twice its height, and the buttons and icons spread out more (Figure 10.6).

FIGURE 10.6 The expanded taskbar

You can resize the taskbar even larger if you like, but double-height is usually enough. (Notice that you are losing workspace on your screen when you make the taskbar larger.) To return the taskbar to its original size, just drag the top border down.

Hiding the Taskbar

To have more room on your desktop, or to make a cleaner-looking desktop, you may want to hide the taskbar. When the taskbar is hidden, you can display it simply by pointing at the bottom of the desktop.

To hide the taskbar:

1 Right-click in an empty area of the taskbar.

2 From the short-cut menu, select **Properties**.

3 In the Taskbar Properties dialog box, click Auto Hide to unselect it.

4 Click OK. The taskbar is hidden.

To turn off Auto Hide, just repeat this process.

11

ENHANCING AND MAINTAINING YOUR SYSTEM

. . . .

As you work with your computer, you will probably add to your system from time to time. And you will need to take care of that system. In this chapter you'll learn how to work with Windows 98 to add programs and hardware, to keep your system running smoothly, and to back up your files for safety.

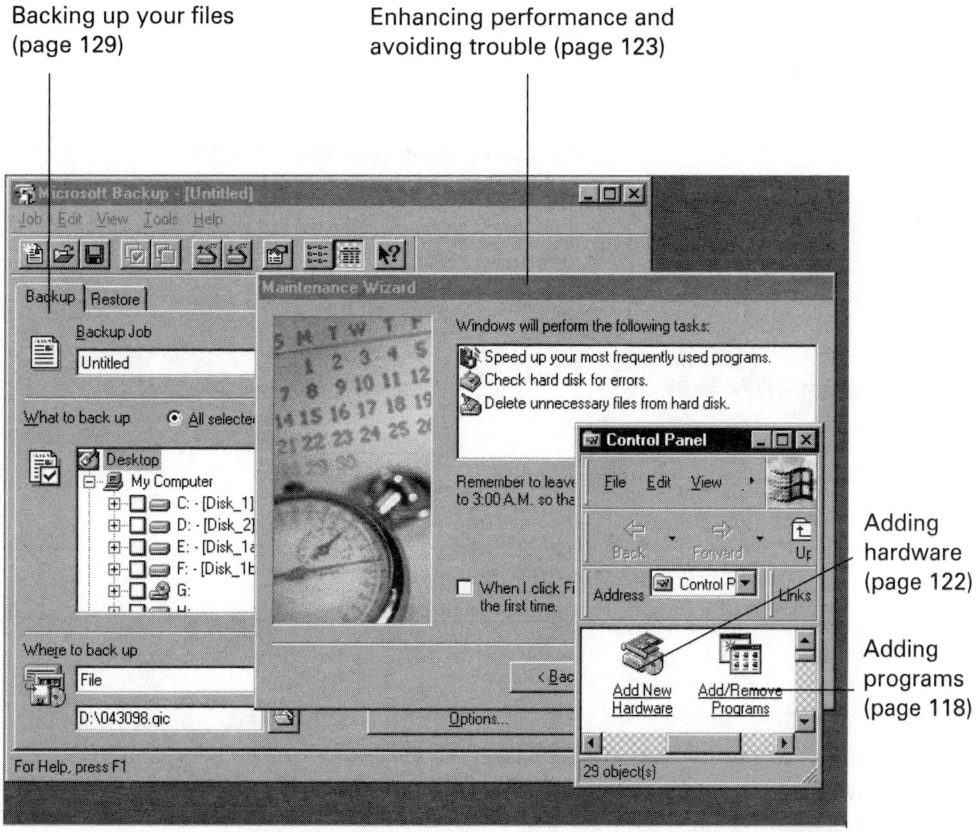

Backing up your files (page 129)

Enhancing performance and avoiding trouble (page 123)

Adding hardware (page 122)

Adding programs (page 118)

FIGURE 11.1 Window 98 provides tools for enhancing and maintaining your system

ADDING PROGRAMS

As you use your computer, you'll occasionally want to add new programs. Most programs handle their own installation—you just get them started, and they do the rest, occasionally asking you for some necessary information.

Preparing for Installation

It's important to be sure your computer is ready for the new program. Programs all have minimum requirements—the resources they need to install and run. The main requirements are for:

- processor speed
- memory
- hard disk space

Some programs also have minimum requirements for CD-ROM speed and monitor resolution, among other things.

Before you install a program, make sure your computer system meets the requirements. The most common installation problem regarding system requirements is not having enough space on your hard disk.

Installing Programs

It is also a good idea to close any open programs before you install. Some installation programs require this.

Once you are ready to install, follow these steps:

1 Insert the program's install (or only) disk in the appropriate disk drive.

2 Select Start ➤ Settings ➤ Control Panel. The Control Panel window opens (Figure 11-2).

 The Control Panel is a set of utilities you use to change settings for your programs (including Windows 98) and your hardware. I used two of these utilities earlier in this book—Date/Time and Display, though I did not open them from the Control Panel.

3 Open the Add/Remove Programs utility.

4 In the dialog box, click Install.

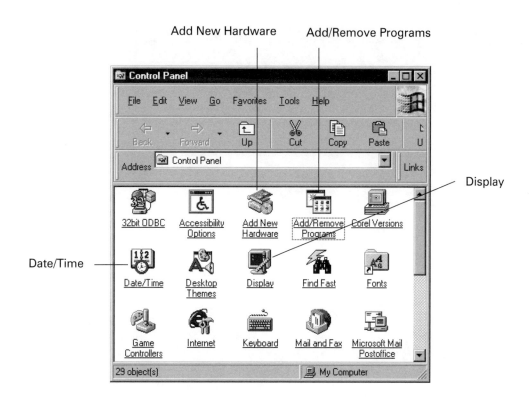

FIGURE 11.2   The Control Panel window

Follow the instructions that display on your screen. Pay attention to the instructions—they may ask you to perform a certain action, such as restarting your computer. These instructions are important for the successful completion of the installation process.

The installation instructions with some programs may tell you to use the Run command on the Start menu, and give you the name of the file that starts the installation. To install from the Run command, follow these instructions:

1   Select Start ➤ Run. The Run dialog box appears (Figure 11-3).

2   Type the installation file location and name in the Run box, or use the Browse button to find the file.

3   Press Enter, and follow the instructions on your screen.

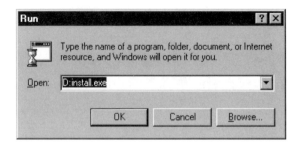

FIGURE 11.3 The Run dialog box

Installing Windows Components

Windows 98 includes a wide variety of components, such as the accessory programs. Many of these are optional—they are available on the installation CD-ROM, but not automatically installed.

For example, the CD-ROM contains many language support components, but not all of them are included in the standard Windows 98 installation. If you want to use one of these components, you will need to add it.

If you want to install one of these components, or if you want to see what components are available, follow these steps:

1 Insert the Windows 98 installation CD-ROM in your CD-ROM drive.

2 From the Control Panel window, open the Add/Remove Programs utility.

3 In the dialog box, select the Windows Setup tab. Windows checks to see what components you have installed, and then displays a list of components (Figure 11-4).

The check boxes in the Components list indicate how much of the component is installed:

• An empty checkbox means that the component is not installed.

• A shaded, marked checkbox means that part of the component is installed.

• A white, marked checkbox means that all of the component is installed.

Components list

Partial installation

Complete
installation

Details button

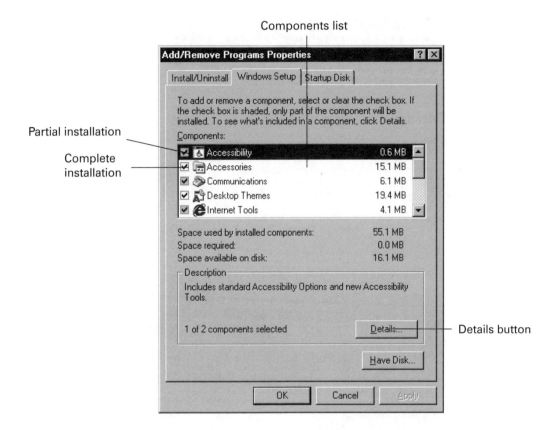

FIGURE 11.4   The Windows Setup tab in the Add/Remove Programs Properties dialog

You can choose what to install by using the detail listings for each component.

4   To see what is included in a component, select it and click the Details button.
A dialog box shows what is selected in the component, and what isn't.

5   To add a component, check it.

6   Click OK.

7   When you are back at the Add/Remove Programs Properties
dialog box, click OK. The new components are installed.

ADDING HARDWARE

Windows 98 makes it easier than ever to add new hardware, such as a new modem, monitor, or printer, to your system.

Installing Printers

To install a new printer, follow these instructions:

1 Connect the printer to the computer.

2 Open the Printers folder from the Control Panel folder (Figure 11-5).

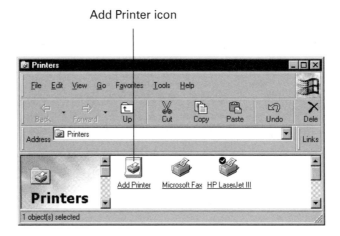

FIGURE 11.5 The Printers folder

3 Open the Add Printer utility. The Add Printer Wizard starts.

4 Follow the instructions in the wizard, as it installs the new printer.

Installing Other Hardware

Hardware devices are continually getting easier to install. A few years ago Plug and Play was introduced, and now there is the easiest standard of all: Universal Serial Bus (USB).

To install a USB device, your computer needs to have a USB port. If it does, just plug the device in—that's it.

To install a new Plug and Play device, follow these steps:

1 Shut down the computer and turn off the power.

2 Connect the device to the computer.

3 Turn the computer on. Windows determines what type of device it is, and installs the appropriate software.

To install other hardware devices, complete these steps:

1 Close all open programs.

2 Connect the device to the computer.

3 Open the Add New Hardware utility from the Control Panel. The Add New Hardware Wizard starts.

4 Follow the instructions in the wizard, as it installs the software for the new hardware device.

 One of the new features of Windows 98 enables you to run more than one monitor from your computer, so your desktop can span multiple monitors.

ENHANCING PERFORMANCE AND AVOIDING TROUBLE

As with anything, your computer will perform better and give you less trouble if you take care of it. Taking care of Windows 98 is easy, with scheduled maintenance tasks, resources on the Web, and wizards to help you.

Many of the Windows 98 tools for taking care of your system are available by selecting Start ➤ Programs ➤ Accessories ➤ System Tools (Figure 11-6).

Disk Defragmenter

As files are added, changed, moved, and deleted, your hard disk becomes fragmented. Disk space is not used efficiently, and the computer requires more time to access those files, meaning that programs run slower.

The Disk Defragmenter utility rearranges the files on your hard disk to use disk space more efficiently, speeding up your programs.

FIGURE 11.6 The System Tools submenu

To run Disk Defragmenter, follow these steps:

1 Select Start ➤ Programs ➤ Accessories ➤ System Tools ➤ Disk Defragmenter.

2 Make sure the disk drive you want to defragment displays in the dialog box.

3 Click OK. Disk Defragmenter starts defragmenting your disk.

4 For a visual representation of its progress, click the Details button.

Defragmenting your hard disk can take some time, depending on factors such as the size of the hard disk, and how fragmented it is. When Disk Defragmenter is done, it asks if you want to defragment another drive. If you don't, just click No.

ScanDisk

As you use your computer, it is possible for errors to develop in the way files and folders are stored on your hard disk. In addition, physical errors can occur on the surface of the disk. These errors can interfere with hard disk performance.

The ScanDisk utility checks your hard disk for errors, and can correct some of the errors it finds. It can not fix physical damage on your hard disk, but it can prevent your system from using the damaged space in the future.

ScanDisk can perform two kinds of tests on your disk:

- **Standard**—checking files and folders for errors.
- **Thorough**—checking files, folders, and disk surface for errors.

To run the ScanDisk utility, complete these steps:

1   Select Start ➤ Programs ➤ Accessories ➤ System Tools ➤ ScanDisk.

2   Make sure the disk drive you want to check is selected in the window (Figure 11-7).

Standard test

Thorough test

Automatic
fix setting

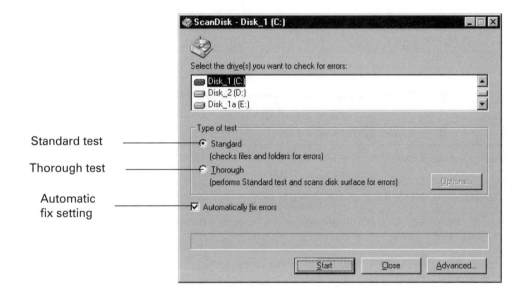

FIGURE 11.7   The ScanDisk window

3   If you want to do a thorough test, which also checks the disk surface (and takes longer to do), select that option.

4   Click Start. ScanDisk checks the disk, then displays a report on what it found, and what it fixed, if anything. If ScanDisk finds any errors, and is not set to fix errors automatically, it will ask you whether to fix them.

5   Click OK. In the ScanDisk dialog box you can select another drive to check. When you're done, click Close.

NOTE If Windows 98 is shut down improperly (for example, your computer loses power, or it locks up and has to be restarted), ScanDisk will run automatically when you restart, to check for disk errors.

Disk Cleanup

Over time, your hard disk accumulates files that you do not need any more: cached Web pages you have visited, files in the Recycle Bin, and so on. The Disk Cleanup utility can recognize many of these types of files, and can get rid of them, making more hard disk space available.

To run Disk Cleanup, follow these steps:

1 Select Start ➤ Programs ➤ Accessories ➤ System Tools ➤ Disk Cleanup.

2 Make sure the disk drive you want to clean up appears in the dialog box.

3 Click OK. Disk Cleanup reviews the files on your hard disk (Figure 11.8).

4 The Disk Cleanup dialog box shows what kinds of types can be deleted, and how much disk space you'll save.

5 If you want to keep any group of files from being deleted, clear its checkbox.

6 Click OK. The files are deleted.

Scheduling Windows 98 Utilities

Windows 98 gives you options for scheduling maintenance and other tasks, so they run automatically.

The Maintenance Wizard utility will automatically run Disk Defragmenter, ScanDisk, and Disk Cleanup on a schedule that you set up. It is a handy way to keep your computer tuned up. Open it from the System Tools menu, choose the schedule, and it's ready.

The Task Scheduler enables you to choose when and how to automatically run programs and utilities. Open the Task Scheduler icon in the taskbar, and let the Scheduled Tasks Wizard lead you through the steps to set up the tasks you want to run (Figure 11-9).

System File Checker

The System File Checker makes sure that your operating system files have not been corrupted. If it finds any corrupted files, it can restore them.

Files to delete

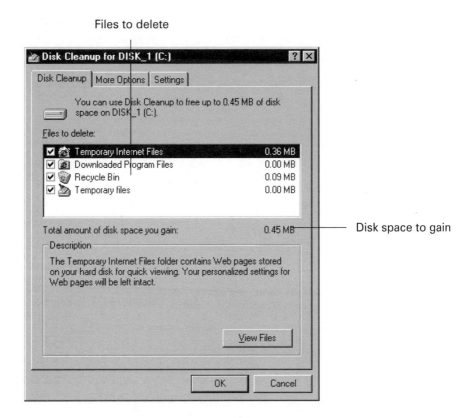

FIGURE 11.8 Disk Cleanup dialog box

Task Scheduler

FIGURE 11.9 The Task Scheduler icon

To run the System File Checker, follow these steps:

1 Select Start ➤ Programs ➤ Accessories ➤ System Tools ➤ System File Checker (or Select Start ➤ Run, type **sfc** and press Enter).

2   Click Start in the dialog box. The utility checks your system files. If any files have been corrupted, System File Checker lets you know, and offers you the option of replacing them with the correct file.

3   When you are done with the utility, click the Close button.

Windows Update

Windows Update is a feature that enables you to get the most up-to-date Windows 98 system files and device drivers from a single location on the Web.

To use Windows Update, complete these steps:

1   Select Start ➤ Windows Update. Internet Explorer opens, and displays the Windows Update home page.

2   Select the Product Updates link.

You can now use the Device Drivers and System Updates feature to determine what can be updated on your computer. You choose what items you want to update, and the appropriate files are downloaded to your computer and installed.

Good Housekeeping

A good way to enhance your system's performance (and your own) is to keep your files current and well-organized. Just as you should get rid of paper files you no longer need, and keep the files you use organized, you should practice "good house-keeping" with your computer files as well.

- **Delete files you don't need.** Files tend to pile up, particularly e-mail messages, both sent and received. (Don't forget to empty the folder with deleted e-mail files, just as you empty the Recycle Bin.)

- **Save or back up files you rarely use,** but want to keep for future reference. You can back up files on removable media (floppy disk, backup tape, and so on) and then delete them from your hard disk.

- **Organize the files you use in folders and subfolders** so that you can find them quickly and easily. Letting files pile up in one folder becomes very inefficient. (For example, a My Documents folder with 350 files in it is not a very useful filing system.)

Good housekeeping should also be taken literally. The more dust in your CPU, the main "box" of your computer, the more heat it retains. Dirt and dust in your keyboard eventually prevent it from working properly. You should keep your computer system covered when it is not in use, and you should use proper cleaning tools and products (available from computer retailers) to keep your computer clean.

BACKING UP YOUR FILES

Sometimes files on your hard disk can be damaged, or even lost. You can accidentally overwrite a file when you are saving. Your hard disk can be damaged, and all your files can be lost.

Backing up your files to removable media (such as floppy disks, Zip disks, or backup tape) insures that you have a backup copy of your files if anything happens to the originals.

How much you back up, and how often, is up to you. I recommend that you back up all the documents you create, and any files your programs use that get added or changed (such as *.ini* files, macro files, and so on).

I also recommend backing up every day. Backup time can vary, depending on your backup device, and the total size of the files you are backing up. But however long it takes, it is still better than trying to recreate a lost or damaged file (which is sometimes impossible).

Creating a New Backup Job

The first time you use the Backup feature, you need to create a new backup job. The Backup Wizard guides you through the process. To create a new backup job, follow these steps:

1   Make sure you have a device to back up to (i.e. large-capacity disk drive or tape drive) connected to your computer, and backup media in the drive.

2   Select Start ➤ Programs ➤ Accessories ➤ System Tools ➤ Backup.

You may get a message that the computer can't find a backup device, asking you if it should install one with the New Hardware Wizard:

- If you have just added a new backup device to your system, click Yes.
- If you are backing up to a device that is already installed, click No.

3   In the dialog box, make sure *Create a new backup job* is selected.

4   Click OK. The Backup Wizard starts, and a dialog box asks what to back up.

5   Select *Back up selected files*, and click the Next button.

6   Use the Explorer-like dialog box to select the files you want to back up. Selecting a drive or folder in the left pane will back up all the contents (including any files and folders you add in the future). To back up only specific files, select them in the right pane.

7   Click the Next button. You can back up all the files in your backup selection, or you can back up only the files that have changed since your last backup. For this procedure, I'll back up all selected files.

8   Make sure *All selected files* is selected, and click the Next button.

9   If you want to change the name of your backup file, type in the new name. (You might find it useful to use the date as the file name.)

10   If your backup location is not displayed, use the folder icon button to browse and select the location.

11   Click the Next button.

12   You can now choose to turn off options that verify your backup, and compress backup data to save space. You probably want to leave those selected.

13   Type a name for the backup job. (The backup job contains all your backup settings. The backup file contains your backed-up data.)

14   Click the Start button. The backup runs.

When the backup is completed, click OK in the message box and in the Progress window, and then close the main Backup window.

Backing Up with an Existing Backup Job

Once you have created a backup job, you can use it each time you back up. To back up using an existing backup job, follow these steps:

1 Make sure you have backup media in the drive to which you back up.

2 Select Start ➤ Programs ➤ Accessories ➤ System Tools ➤ Backup.

3 Select *Open an existing backup job*, then click OK.

4 Select the backup job from the list, then click Open.

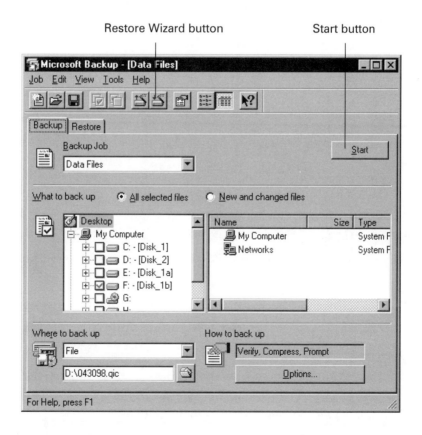

FIGURE 11.10 The Backup Window

The Backup window shows the backup settings you selected when you created the backup job. You can change those settings—for example, which files to back up—in this window.

  Each time you back up, you may want to enter a new backup file name (at the bottom of the Backup window). Then your previous backup file is unchanged, just in case you need something from that particular backup. Every so often you can delete older backup files.

5 When you have changed any settings you want to, click the Start button.

6 If you have changed any settings, a dialog box asks if you want to save the job with the new settings. Click Yes.

7 If you have not changed the backup file name, a dialog box asks if you want to overwrite the existing file.

• If you do want to overwrite the file: click Overwrite.

• If you don't want to overwrite the file: click Cancel, change the file name in the Backup window, and click Start again.

The backup runs. When the backup is completed, click OK in the message box and in the Progress window, and then close the main Backup window.

Restoring Files

If your files are lost, damaged or overwritten, you can restore them—if they have been backed up. When you need to restore a backed-up file, follow these steps:

1 Make sure backup media is in the drive you want to restore from.

2 Select Start ➤ Programs ➤ Accessories ➤ System Tools ➤ Backup.

3 Click the Restore Wizard button in the Backup Window (Figure 11.10).

The Restore Wizard guides you through a process similar to that of the Backup Wizard. You select where you want to restore from, what you want to restore, where you want to restore it to, and how you want to restore.

You can also restore by choosing the Restore tab in the Backup Window and selecting the settings there.

Installing Windows 98

I f your computer does not have Windows 98 installed, you will need to install it. (Computer systems sold since Windows 98 was released will typically have Windows 98 already installed.) In either case, you will also need to register your copy of Windows 98 with Microsoft.

Installing Windows 98

Here are two things you should do in preparation for installing Windows 98:

- If you are having any problems with your computer **hardware**, installing a new operating system will not fix them. Resolve hardware problems before installing Windows 98.

- Back up any critical data files. While there is only a very slim chance that you could lose any of your data when you install a new operating system, it is always best to be safe.

System Requirements

Before you install Windows 98, make sure that your computer meets the minimal system requirements for installing and running windows:

- 486DX / 66 MHz or higher processor.

- 16 MB of memory; more memory improves performance.

- Typical installation requires approximately 195 MB of free hard disk space, but may range between 120 MB to 295 MB, depending on your system configuration and the options you choose to install.

- CD-ROM or DVD-ROM drive (3.5" high-density disks available for additional charge).

- VGA or higher-resolution monitor.

- Microsoft Mouse or compatible pointing device.

Starting the Installation

Installing Windows 98 is a simple process: the installation generally runs itself. You will occasionally be prompted for an action, such as choosing from a set of options, so you need to keep an eye on the process.

To start the installation, insert the Windows 98 CD-ROM (not the CompuWorks CD-ROM) in your computer's CD-ROM drive. The Setup program starts automatically, and the Installation Wizard guides you through the process.

You can choose from four installation options when installing Windows 98:

Typical: This is the most common installation option.

Portable: This option installs features designed especially for portable computer users.

Compact: This option installs the minimum files needed for Windows 98 to run properly.

Custom: This option enables you to install only the Windows 98 components that you want.

Once you have made your choice, the setup process begins. The installation program will copy the necessary files to your computer, make the proper settings for your hardware devices, and configure the system. Along the way you may be asked questions, or be given some information, which will require a response from you. When the process is completed, Windows 98 is operating.

Registering Windows 98

Registering your software is optional, but it is a good idea. Registered users have access to technical support and the Windows Update Web site for the latest in device drivers and system files.

Windows 98 comes with a traditional paper registration card, but also offers online registration, guided by the Registration Wizard. If you have a modem connected to a phone line, you can use this option.

When you install, you are offered the chance to register online. If you want to do it later, just follow these steps:

1   Select Start ➤ Programs ➤ Accessories ➤ System Tools ➤ Welcome to Windows. The Windows 98 Welcome screen displays.

2   In the Contents list, click Register Now. The Registration Wizard starts.

The wizard extracts information from your system, ensuring its accuracy and doing much of the registration work for you. And because the information is submitted to Microsoft electronically, it can be processed faster than using the traditional paper method.

TROUBLESHOOTING

. . . .

As you use Windows 98, there may be times that you encounter technical problems. Windows 98 has included a series of troubleshooters as part of its Help system, to help you diagnose your problem and find a solution to it.

Using Windows 98 Troubleshooters

Troubleshooters are an interactive form of Windows 98 Help. The troubleshooters are wizard utilities that guide you with a series of questions and suggestions, helping you quickly diagnose and solve technical problems.

To run a Windows 98 troubleshooter, follow these steps:

1 From the Start menu, select Help.

2 In the Help window, make sure the Contents tab is selected.

3 Click Troubleshooting, then Windows 98 Troubleshooters.

4 Click the troubleshooter you want to use. The first page of the troubleshooter displays in the right pane.

 If you want to display more of the computer screen while you work with the troubleshooter, click the Hide button in the Help window toolbar to hide the left pane. To display the left pane again, click the Show button.

5 Choose the selection that best describes your problem and click the Next button. Based on your answer, the troubleshooter asks a question.

6 Choose the best answer, then click Next.

The troubleshooter asks more questions as necessary. To back up and answer a question differently, click the Back button. To return to the beginning, click the Start Over button.

When the troubleshooter has enough information, it displays a set of instructions.

7 Follow the instructions. At the bottom of the right pane, the troubleshooter asks if the problem is solved.

8 Click to answer as appropriate.

If you click Yes, the troubleshooter closes. If you click No, the troubleshooter will offer more suggestions, if it has any.

If you want to close the Help window, click the X button in the upper right.

Finding the Right Troubleshooter

In some cases, you might not know which troubleshooter to use. This section lists many common problems and the appropriate troubleshooters to solve them.

Animations, stop playing—Display

Busy signal—The Microsoft Network

Calling card, not working correctly—Modem

Calls, canceled before completed—Modem

Communications program, not working—Modem

Compressed Drive Access error message—DriveSpace 3

Connecting other computers to mine—Networking

Connection Status dialog box, shows error message—The Microsoft Network

Cursor, black screen or black patches surrounding—DirectX

Dial tone not detected message—Modem

Dial-Up Networking connection, can't save password—Modem

Dialog boxes, not centered—Display

Direct Cable Connection, using a high-speed parallel cable—Networking

DirectDraw error messages—DirectX

DriveSpace completed, computer will not start correctly—DriveSpace 3

DriveSpace, fails or stops after 25 percent—DriveSpace 3

Exception 03h in Msvfw32.dll message—DirectX

Filesharing—Networking

Fonts missing or appear different than on screen—Printing

Graphics distorted or incomplete when printed—Printing

Hardware conflict, resolving—Hardware Conflict

International calls, cannot dial—Modem

Internet service provider, slow connection—Modem

Internet, connecting to—Modem

Invalid Page Fault in Kernel32.dll message—Display

Sound, causes computer to restart—Sound

Sound, causes computer to stop responding—Sound

Sound, choppy—DirectX

Sound, distorted or scratchy—Sound

Sound, stops suddenly—Sound

Sounds, appear to play but doesn't—Sound

Sounds, missing from program—Sound

Sounds, not functioning—DirectX

Starting computer, Invalid VxD error message—Startup and Shutdown

Starting Windows 98, computer stops responding—Startup and Shutdown

Starting Windows 98, starts only in safe mode—DirectX

Text, garbled or corrupted on screen—Display

Vertical lines, appear on screen—DirectX

Video, blurry or scrambled—Display

WAV sound playback error detected message—Sound

Window, want to run program in—MS DOS Programs

Wsock32.dll file cannot start message—DirectX

KEYBOARD SHORTCUTS

C

Windows 98 provides keyboard shortcuts for performing many tasks. The shortcut keys can be very convenient, especially when you are doing a lot of data entry and editing—your hands can stay at the keyboard.

Using Keyboard Shortcuts

Keyboard shortcuts are used in this way:

Hold the first key (or keys),

Press the last key, and

Release all the keys.

Most programs that run in windows make use of keyboard shortcuts, and many of the shortcuts are the same, no matter what you are working in. This appendix includes keyboard shortcuts for working in a window, and for working in a dialog box. These tables were taken from the Windows Help feature, and are presented here as a handy reference. The Help feature offers other tables of keyboard shortcuts.

Shortcut Keys in a Window

To	Press
Activate the menu bar in programs	F10
Carry out the corresponding command on the menu	ALT+underlined letter in menu
Close the current window in (MDI) programs	CTRL+F4
Close the current window or quit a program	ALT+F4
Copy	CTRL+C
Cut	CTRL+X
Delete	DELETE
Display Help on the selected dialog box item	F1
Display the current window's system menu	ALT+SPACEBAR

To	Press
Display the shortcut menu for the selected item	SHIFT+F10
Display the Start menu	CTRL+ESC
Display the system menu for MDI programs	ALT+HYPHEN (-)
Paste	CTRL+V
Switch to the window you last used or switch to another	ALT+TAB
Undo	CTRL+Z

Shortcut Keys in Dialog Boxes

To	Press
Cancel the current task	ESC
Click a button if the current control is a button Or Select or clear the check box if the current control is a check box Or Click the option if the current control is an option button	SPACEBAR
Click the corresponding command	ALT+underlined letter
Click the selected button	ENTER
Move backward through options	SHIFT+TAB
Move backward through tabs	CTRL+SHIFT+TAB
Move forward through options	TAB
Move forward through tabs	CTRL+TAB
Open a folder one level up if a folder is selected in the Save As or Open dialog box	BACKSPACE
Open Save In or Look In the Save As or Open dialog box	F4
Refresh the Save As or Open dialog box	F5

How to Use the CompuWorks CD-ROM

The CompuWorks CD-ROM is easy to install and use. Just follow the simple instructions in this appendix, and you'll be on your way.

System Requirements

Before you install the CompuWorks CD-ROM, make sure that your computer meets the minimal system requirements for installing and running the program:

- Pentium 100 or higher
- 8 MB of RAM (16 MB recommended)
- 5 MB free hard disk space
- 4X CD-ROM or DVD-ROM drive
- 8 bit 256 color display, 16 bit or higher recommended
- 800 x 600 screen resolution
- Microsoft Mouse or compatible pointing device

Installing the CompuWorks CD-ROM

To install the CompuWorks CD-ROM program, follow these steps:

1 Insert the CompuWorks CD-ROM into your CD-ROM drive.
2 From the Start menu, select Run. A dialog box appears. If the setup program starts automatically on your computer, go to Step 4.
3 Type: **x:\setup.exe** (where x is the letter of your CD-ROM drive). Click OK
4 Follow the instructions that appear on your screen.

After you have successfully installed the CD-ROM, the program starts automatically.

Uninstalling the CompuWorks CD-ROM

If you decide you no longer want the CompuWorks CD-ROM installed on your hard disk, you can uninstall it. To uninstall the program, follow these steps:

1   From the Start menu, select Programs ➤ CompuWorks ➤ Learn Microsoft Windows 98.

2   Select the option to uninstall, and follow the instructions.

After you have removed the program from your hard disk, it can be reinstalled at any time.

Using the CompuWorks CD-ROM

The CompuWorks CD-ROM interface incorporates a Windows 98-style functionality that is easy to learn and easy to use.

To start the program, just follow these steps:

1   From the Start menu, select Programs ➤ CompuWorks ➤ Learn Microsoft Windows 98.

2   Run the program.

The CompuWorks interface is similar to a Windows Explorer or Help window. The right pane is the media window, where the demo movie clips play. The left pane is where you choose what to play.

Playing a Movie Clip

When the Contents tab is selected, the navigation tree displays, showing the structure of the course:

- The book icons represent the sections of the course. The folder icons represent the lessons. The document icons represent the demo movie clips.

- Click the + and – symbols to open and close the section and lesson icons.

- Play a clip by selecting it and clicking the Play button.

When the Index tab is selected, all of the clips on the CD-ROM are listed in alphabetical order. The clips can be played from the Index tab just as they can be played from the Contents tab.

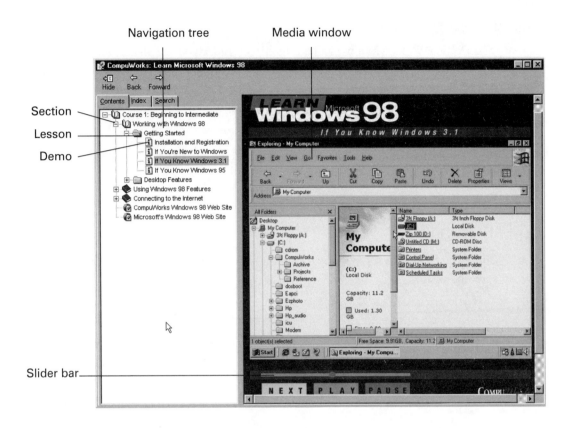

Navigation tree   Media window

Section

Lesson

Demo

Slider bar

FIGURE D.1 The CompuWorks CD-ROM interface

 If you are a proficient Windows 95 user, you can skip the movie clips marked with a star.

Controlling a Movie Clip

When a movie clip plays in the media window, VCR-style controls display below it, with these controls:

- **Next**—Opens the next movie in that section.
- **Play**—Starts the current movie.
- **Pause**—Stops the movie
- **The slider bar**—Drag this left or right to move to any part of the movie.

Controlling the Window

The CompuWorks window can be moved, resized, maximized, and minimized like any window in Windows 98. You can switch between it and your desktop and any programs you are running. To switch, just click a program button in the toolbar, or use the Alt+Tab keyboard shortcut.

The Hide button in the toolbar is similar to the one in Windows Help:

- **Hide**—removes the left pane from view, and changes to a Show button.
- **Show**—displays the left pane.

Technical Support

Support is available for Windows 98, and for the CompuWorks CD-ROM and reference guide.

If you are a registered Windows 98 user, you will have information from Microsoft about getting technical support by phone, by fax, and online.

You can connect to Windows 98 information online directly from the Compu-Works CD-ROM interface, which includes an icon for the CompuWorks Windows 98 Web site, and for Microsoft's Windows 98 Web site.

For telephone support on the CompuWorks CD-ROM and this reference guide, call:

CompuWorks Technical Support

612-559-5301

Monday through Friday, 9 AM to 5 PM, Central Time

GLOSSARY

Active Channel—*See* channel.

Active Desktop—A feature that displays the desktop like a Web page, and enables you to put active Web content on the desktop.

address—*See* URL.

Address bar—Provides a text box in which you enter the address of a file on the Internet, or a file or folder on your computer, or on a network. When you enter an address in the Address bar, the file or folder at that address opens. *See also* AutoComplete.

AutoComplete—An Address bar feature that finishes typing a previously used address.

browse—To view files on the Internet, on your computer, or on a network.

browser—*See* Web browser.

cache—A folder on your computer used for temporarily storing files.

channel—A Web site specially designed to deliver content to your computer. You can subscribe to a channel and set up a schedule for how and when the content is automatically delivered to your computer. *See also* Channel bar.

Channel bar—A list of the channels installed on your computer.

Classic style—The Windows 95 style of desktop display.

CD-ROM(Compact Disc Read-Only Memory)—Also called a "CD" or "compact disc." A high-capacity storage medium often used for delivering multimedia programs and software applications. Using CD-ROMs requires that you have a CD-ROM drive, found on almost all new computers.

content provider—A publisher of content (including news, weather, business reports, entertainment) on the Internet.

Control Panel—The tools that enable you to change your hardware and software settings.

default—The standard setting or preference in a software program or operating system. Such settings can often be changed or personalized by the user.

desktop—Your workspace on the computer screen. *See also* Active Desktop.

dialog box—A window that requires your input to complete an action. Your input might come in the form of entering text, selecting options, or just clicking OK.

disk drive—A storage device on your computer for files. Computers have a hard disk (often labeled C:) and can also have drives for floppy disks, CD-ROMs, and other storage devices.

document—A file created by a software application. Examples of documents include word-processing files, spreadsheets, and graphics.

download—To copy files from one computer to another connected by modem or network. For example, files copied from the Web are "downloaded" to your computer.

drive—*See* disk drive.

e-mail—Electronic messaging from one person to another over the Internet or a network.

Explorer bar—An optional interface feature in Internet Explorer. You can view Channels, Favorites, History, or Search information in the Explorer bar, while hyperlinked content appears in the browser window.

favorite—A Web page that you visit often, or a file or folder you use often. Addresses of favorites are stored in a list, enabling you to easily access the favorite.

file—An application or document stored on a disk.

folder—A storage location on a disk for files and other folders.

HTML (Hypertext Markup Language)—The code used for creating most Web pages. A Web browser interprets and displays HTML documents. *See also* Web page.

home page—The main page of a Web site.

hyperlink—A picture, navigational button, or text that takes you from one location to another when you click it. Hyperlinks can be within a Web page, from page to page, or to another Web site.

icon—A small picture representing a location or function of your computer.

Internet—A network of computers around the world with millions of sources of information. Internet access enables you to download information, send and receive e-mail and newsgroup messages, and browse the World Wide Web. *See also* World Wide Web.

Internet service provider (ISP)—A company that provides access to the Internet.

intranet—A private network, accessed only by members of a company or organization. An intranet can be connected to the Internet.

LAN—*See* local area network.

local area network (LAN)—A group of connected computers in the same location.

menu—A list of functions that appears at the top of most windows, most often in menu bars or dropdown lists.

modem—A device that transmits data between computers across phone lines.

multimedia—Media containing a combination of text, pictures, sound, video, or animation.

My Computer—A file and system management utility, represented and accessed by an icon on the desktop.

network—A group of two or more computers that are connected. *See also* workgroup.

offline—Not connected to a network or the Internet.

operating system—The software that controls applications and hardware on your computer.

path—Directions you give to your computer to find a specific location on a computer or network. The path is like an address for a file; it includes (as necessary) the computer name, disk drive label, folder names, and a file name.

Profile—Personalized settings for a Windows 98 user, including color schemes, screen savers, and desktop backgrounds.

Refresh—To display or redisplay the most recent version of a Web page or window.

right-click—To click with the secondary mouse button, typically the right button.

search engine—A tool that helps you find information on the Web. You can access several search engines by clicking the Search button in the Internet Explorer toolbar.

server—A computer that controls access to a network and its shared resources.

shortcut—A copy of an icon that enables you to conveniently access a program or document.

shortcut menu—The menu that appears when you right-click an object.

subscribe—A request for Internet Explorer to periodically check a Web page for new content.

taskbar—A tool, found at the bottom of your screen, for navigating your computer and opening programs.

text box—An area for entering text.

toolbar—A set of buttons representing an application's common functions or commands.

URL (Uniform Resource Locator)—The location, or address, of a file on the Internet.

wallpaper—The background of your desktop. In Windows 98, you can choose from a solid color, a selected bitmap, a Web page, or your own files.

Web—*See* World Wide Web.

Web browser—A program that interprets and displays HTML documents, enabling you to explore the World Wide Web. Internet Explorer is the Web browser included with Windows 98.

Web page—A document on the World Wide Web, often part of a larger Web site.

Web site—A group of documents published together on the World Wide Web.

Web-style—A viewing option in Windows 98 that enables you to navigate your computer in the same way you navigate the World Wide Web.

Window—The model for viewing and working with information, on which the Windows 98 operating system is based. A portion of your screen displays an open document, or the contents of a folder or disk.

Windows Explorer—A program used for managing files and folders on your computer and network.

Wizard—A tool that leads you through an automated process.

World Wide Web—The graphical, multimedia portion of the Internet. Often referred to as the Web. *See also* Internet, Web page.

INDEX

• • • • • • • • • • • • • • • • • • • •